LEADING THE SALES TEAM

LEADING THE SALES TEAM

❖

David Hillier

Gower

© David Hillier 1994

The materials that appear in this book, other than those quoted from prior sources, may be reproduced for education/training activities. There is no requirement to obtain special permission for such uses.

This permission statement is limited to reproduction of materials for educational or training events. Systematic or large-scale reproduction or distribution – or inclusion of items in publication for sale – may be carried out only with prior written permission from the publisher.

Published by
Gower Publishing Limited
Gower House
Croft Road
Aldershot
Hampshire GU11 3HR
England

Gower
Old Post Road
Brookfield
Vermont 05036
USA

David Hillier has asserted his right under the Copyright, Designs and Patents Act 1988 to be identified as the author of this work.

British Library Cataloguing in Publication Data
Hillier, David
Leading the Sales Team
I. Title
658.85

ISBN 0–566–07494–X

Library of Congress Cataloging-in-Publication Data
Hillier, David
Leading the sales team/David Hillier.
p. cm.
Companion volume to the author's: Training the sales team.
ISBN 0–566–07494–X
1. Selling—Personnel management.   2. Sales personnel—Training of.   I. Hillier, David. Training the sales team.   II. Title.
HF5439.5.H55   1994
658.3'1245—dc20
94-15192
CIP

Typeset in 11 point Garamond Light by Poole Typesetting (Wessex) Limited
and printed in Great Britain by Bookcraft Ltd, Midsomer Norton

CONTENTS

List of tables and figures	vii
Preface	ix
How to use this book	xi

1 What is leadership? — 1
Defining leadership – Four sources of leadership – Summary

2 Sales leadership in practice — 11
Managing by goals – Building the sales team – Applying leadership styles – Managing change – Managing difficult staff – Summary

3 Motivation — 21
An introduction to motivation – Understanding motivation through needs – A simple theory of needs – Analysing your staff's needs – Appealing to your staff's needs – The theory of roles – Summary – Appendix: Theories of motivation

4 Putting motivation to work — 33
Motivating through organization – Clear duties, responsibilities and aims – The job description – The sales manual – Clear expectations, standards and grounds for success – Daily working structure – Monitoring performance – Summary

5 Goal-setting, reviews, promotion and discipline — 41
Constructive goal-setting – Make goal-setting work! – Reviews – Handling complaints and grievances – Discipline – Promotions – Team structure – Summary

6 Communication — 53
How to communicate – Managing the sales meeting – Summary

7 Commission schemes and prizes — 59
Introduction – Sales commission schemes – Prizes and competitions

8 Evaluating the sales team 65
What to assess – How to measure performance – Other forms of assessment – Putting your assessment to work – Summary

9 Administration and organization 77
Assessing your administration – Planning improvements – How to improve administration – Keeping and using records – Computerization – Summary

10 Customer service 85
Benefits of customer service – Developing customer service – Targeting customers – The customer service questionnaire – Gaining referrals – After-sales service – Handling complaints – Conclusion: looking to the future

11 Recruiting the sales team – finding the right people 93
Staff turnover – good or bad? – Why do staff leave? – Identifying your requirements – The recruitment specification – Sourcing – Summary

12 Recruiting the sales team – interviewing and offering 103
Planning the interview process – The application form – How to interview – Questions to ask – Information to prepare – Reviewing your interviews – The second interview – Taking up references – Tests – Making offers – Making rejections – Conclusion

13 Troubleshooting 111
Lack of motivation and poor morale – Falling sales – Only one or two high performers in the team – Staff not working long/hard enough – Staff not doing their work thoroughly – High staff turnover

14 Managing difficult staff 123
Understanding difficult behaviour – Typical problems – Disruptive behaviour – Discipline – How to avoid disruptive behaviour – Conclusion

Conclusion 131
Index 135

LIST OF TABLES AND FIGURES

TABLES

2.1	Leadership styles	17
8.1	Daily figure sheet	69
8.2	Quarterly figure sheet	70
8.3	Monthly ratios	70
9.1	Assessment and implementation chart	78

FIGURES

3.1	Staff motivation questionnaire	25
8.1	Staff self-assessment form	74
10.1	Customer service questionnaire	89

PREFACE

Over the past six years I have had the opportunity to work with a wide variety of successful businesses who have not only survived the recent recession, but have actually seen their turnover and profits increase. Of course, each company was in its own way unique, and each sold different products, different services. But all had two factors in common: successful sales leadership and successful sales training. Of the two, sales leadership must come first. In fact, the ability to *lead*, that is, the ability to inspire, motivate, direct and organize the sales force, and above all, the ability to help the sales force make money, is probably the single most important factor in determining the success of any business today.

This book will help you become more aware of your own ability to lead and motivate the sales force. It will give you realistic, practical advice on how to troubleshoot problems, cope with difficult staff, introduce and manage change. It will suggest ways of getting more out of your commission scheme, review structure and sales meetings. It will help you recruit, retain and direct the best staff for your team. But, above all else, its aim is to help you improve the actual performance of your sales force so that your staff are happier, work harder and earn more for you and themselves than they thought possible.

The companion volume to this book, *Training the Sales Team*, will show you ways of putting effective sales skills into practice and developing the abilities of your staff.

David Hillier

HOW TO USE THIS BOOK

This book is written to be a practical guide to sales leadership. Use it in the workplace to help tackle and solve the everyday problems and challenges of leading the sales team, and to suggest fresh ideas for future growth and strategy. It is divided into 14 chapters, each one covering an aspect or function of sales leadership. Each chapter is in turn broken down into shorter, easily digestible sections. Although the chapters do follow on from each other, I have provided extensive cross-references so that you can read the book in whatever order you find most helpful, or simply 'dip in' at points of interest.

1

WHAT IS LEADERSHIP?

This first chapter will help you come to your own understanding of the essence of sales *leadership*, as opposed to simple management, and how it can be applied in your organization to achieve the best results. Many of the themes and ideas presented here are developed later in the book or in its companion volume, *Training the Sales Team*. If a particular idea interests you, feel free to use the cross-references and index to move around the book in any way which suits. Subjects covered in this chapter are:

- Defining leadership
- Four sources of leadership
    - Personal qualities
    - Treating staff
    - Position within the organization
    - Ways of working.

DEFINING LEADERSHIP

There is no single definition of leadership which is 100 per cent accurate. Leadership, like sales, is defined by results: a good leader is someone who successfully *leads people* – whether he or she conforms to a definition or a set of qualities or activities is, to a certain extent, incidental. However, there are some qualities and ways of working which many good and successful leaders do have in common, and there are certain approaches which make success more likely.

Let's start by examining two, quite different, definitions of leadership which I think are particularly helpful:

> **Leadership is the ability to inspire others to do willingly what you want them to do.**
>
> **Leaders must provide well-being, organization and a set of beliefs for their team.**

The first definition tells us the fundamentals of what leaders do: first of all, they have clear *goals* – there are things they want people to do; secondly, they do not just *make* people do things, they get people to actually want to do them of their own accord – people *identify* with their leaders' goals; thirdly, there is an *inspirational* quality in the way leaders deal with their team.

The second definition views leadership from a different perspective. It does not say what you must do to achieve your goals, but what you must do for your team so that your goals can be achieved. First of all, you must provide them with both *material* and *emotional well-being* – you must give your staff the opportunity and the means to earn good commission, and must make them feel good about themselves. Secondly, you must provide the *organization*, the *structure*, the *sense of direction* necessary for success. Thirdly, you must give them a *shared set of values and goals*.

FOUR SOURCES OF LEADERSHIP

One of the best ways to understand leadership in practice is to break it down into areas or *sources*. There are four sources of leadership which we will deal with here, each one essentially for overall success:

- Personal qualities
- Treating staff
- Position within the organization
- Ways of working.

These four topics form the four headings for the rest of this chapter. They will give us a detailed understanding of what makes an effective sales leader and how that person works with their staff and company to achieve the best results. In Chapter 2 we examine some specific, practical examples of sales leadership.

PERSONAL QUALITIES

No two leaders are the same. Often it is their very individualism, their extraordinariness as it were, which makes them such inspiring and successful leaders. Alexander the Great, Napoleon Bonaparte or, in the world of business, Henry Ford, Lee Iacocca and John Harvey-Jones are not 'average' people. Nevertheless, there are certain qualities which most leaders do, on analysis, seem to have in common. Certainly in the context of sales leadership, the following are all vital for success:

- Vision
- Goal-orientation
- Ability to see the whole picture
- Strength of character
- Confidence
- Understanding
- Compassion and concern
- Indifference to popularity
- Sense of humour
- Belief and commitment
- Ability to inspire
- Tendency to work hard
- Positive, optimistic attitude
- Unselfishness
- Enthusiasm
- Assertiveness
- Decisiveness
- Fine critical faculties/'wisdom'
- Excellent memory
- Interest in people
- Excellent communication skills
- Attention to detail

- Ability to use power wisely
- Consistency
- Single-mindedness, but also willingness to adapt, change.

This is a long list, which is hardly surprising. Sales leadership is one of the most complex and challenging forms of management. There cannot be just one or two factors which will guarantee a consistently successful sales leader. Most of the qualities we have listed are self-evident, but perhaps some need explanation.

Vision, goal-orientation, strength of character, belief and commitment, enthusiasm

A leader must have clear goals, be able to convey them to those around him/her, and stick to them through adversity. If you do not have goals, you have nothing to lead your staff towards. This subject is covered in 'Managing by goals' in Chapter 2.

Confidence

Leaders must have confidence in themselves, their goals and their people. A great leader will inspire his or her team to have that confidence not only in him/her, but in themselves.

Understanding, compassion and concern, interest in people

Leaders must understand and care for the people they are leading. If you have no interest in them, you will not be able to motivate them or resolve their problems.

Indifference to popularity

Good leaders are almost by definition 'popular'. They will always be looking for ways to inspire more enthusiasm for their leadership and their goals. However, good leaders will never make a bad decision just to win favour or to satisfy their personal desire to be liked.

Ability to inspire

Perhaps the single most important quality. As a leader, you will inspire people either to believe in you personally or to believe in your goals. In sales leadership, all that is necessary is that your staff believe in and identify with your goals, which might be better sales figures, greater team spirit, higher standards of professionalism. To a large extent, your ability to inspire will depend on your ability to convey your own *enthusiasm* in an understandable manner, and convey the essential *value* of your goals as things good in themselves.

Unselfishness

Sales leaders should never put their own, selfish needs over those of the team. Staff will not see their treatment as 'fair' if you treat yourself indulgently.

Tendency to work hard

A basic law of leadership is that no one will work harder than the leader. This is not quite true in sales, where an individual may be self-motivated (providing the commission scheme makes it worthwhile), but if you want to be an effective leader, you must always set an example.

Attention to detail

In sales, the money is often made, the deal won or lost, in the small detail. Unless you are able to look at things more closely than your staff you will not see their mistakes.

Excellent memory

The most awesome sales managers are those who never forget anything, who will remember conversations from months before, who will remember sales leads, contacts, details. As the sales manager, you are probably the only person in your team who sees the whole picture. You therefore need to remember enough details in order to identify opportunities or team-wide problems or to see the connections between your various markets. Sales managers must be able to remember as much detail about each person's work as possible, so they can truly talk to each person about their work (and meaningfully praise and criticize), and spot inconsistencies: salespeople lose respect for managers who forget what they've been told and who are, consequently, easy to mislead.

Decisiveness

The worst decision is almost always the one you avoid making. Staff sense indecisiveness and interpret it as either weakness or lack of goals: both are fatal to good leadership.

Fairness

Management involves deciding how to praise, reward or discipline staff, how to settle disputes, how to organize the workforce. The point to grasp is that your decisions must be *seen* to be fair. It is no good being fair if you impose your decisions in ways which appear unfair or ill-contrived.

Single-mindedness, but willingness to change

Leaders should never give up as long as they have a chance of winning, but they have to recognize when to change either their tactics or their goals. Leaders should not be afraid of change provided it does not reduce their staff's confidence. A weak or insecure leader will stick with policies which no longer work.

Ability to use power wisely

No one respects leaders who abuse their position, or use their power to bully or coerce people needlessly. Leaders should respect the people they lead. They should also be happy to delegate power and responsibility when appropriate.

Excellent communication skills

None of the qualities we have considered will be of any use to you if you cannot communicate them to your staff. You need to be able to explain yourself and your goals in ways which are *clear, rational, emotional,* and above all *persuasive*. (For more on communication, see Chapter 6.)

TREATING STAFF

Too much attention to the qualities of sales leadership can make us see leadership as a solitary pursuit. Nothing could be further from the truth: leadership is essentially *leadership of people*. A person can have as many or as few leadership qualities as you like, but if he or she cannot work with people, he or she will fail. Almost all the qualities we have just reviewed should be interpreted in relationship to the people you will be leading: how can you understand *them*? how can you inspire *them*? how can you discipline *them*? how can you help *them* to identify with *your* goals?

This section explores the practical ways you can relate these qualities to the people in your sales team. The points we will cover are as follows:

- Match your goals to your situation.
- Match your leadership to your situation.
- Signpost your objectives and decisions.
- Praise your staff and recognize their achievements.
- Give constructive criticism.
- Consult your staff.
- Give clear, structured tasks.

- Help, advise and support.
- Develop the right relationship.
- Discipline and reward.

Match your goals to your situation

Always make sure your goals are appropriate to your situation. A poor sales manager will aim to achieve too much or too little, or will have goals which are not shared by either his team or his company. This last point is crucial, for if your goals are not in harmony with your superiors, you will not have the confidence and authority to act.

Within your team, you must constantly reappraise your goals: are they appropriate? are they achievable? are they set high enough to motivate, but not too high to demotivate? and, most important of all, does your team believe in them? If they do not, you must look for ways of bridging this gap immediately. Maybe your staff don't see how your goals will benefit them? or perhaps they don't think achieving these goals is worth the effort required? Understanding and harnessing human motivation is dealt with more fully in Chapters 3, 4 and 5.

Match your leadership to your situation

You also need to match your style of leadership. What may be an appropriate way of talking to a new trainee will not work with an experienced senior salesperson. What may work in a crisis, may not work in a boom. The many different styles of leadership are considered in Chapter 2.

Signpost your objectives and decisions

Always keep your staff informed: make them aware of the possibility of change before it happens; keep them regularly updated on sales figures, market news and so on; confirm decisions and announcements in writing. All of this improves team spirit, shows your staff you have a sense of direction, and reinforces their sense of security and confidence. For more on this topic, see Chapter 6.

Praise your staff and recognize their achievements

Never be grudging with your praise – but only praise sincerely and for genuine reasons. Always be keen to praise staff in front of other people and other managers – nothing makes a person feel better. When you praise, adopt the following approach:

- Tell the person you are pleased with them.
- Tell him/her why you are pleased (what they have done/said/achieved etc.).
- Pause, and let the person enjoy your praise.

Always *thank* staff for working or trying hard. Show them you appreciate their effort. Staff know you don't have to thank them (it is a job, after all), and because of that they will value it all the more – and will act to earn more thanks.

Give constructive criticism

Only in extreme situations should you bluntly criticize your staff. However, if they have done wrong, you must let them know; constructive criticism is more effective because it shows the person how they can do better next time. Here are some suggestions:

- Ask the person what he/she thinks they have done wrong.
- Ask him/her how they think they could do better.

- Tell the person what he or she does well.
- Point out the area which lets them down/where they could do better.
- Explain how they can improve.
- Ask if they agree.
- Praise them.

Consult your staff

To be a good leader you don't need to have all the answers. There are many situations when it is better to ask your staff, rather than take a guess. If there are new goals to achieve, or difficult sales-objections to overcome, often your staff will suggest fresh and effective methods. If one of your staff asks you to solve a difficult problem, never be afraid to ask him/her how he thinks it should be tackled.

Staff will more willingly work towards a goal which they think they have helped formulate. For this reason it is often a good idea to appear to consult with staff even when you know what you want to achieve.

Give clear, structured tasks

People cannot be inspired to do anything if they do not know what you want them to do. Start by defining your goals clearly to yourself (what is it you want your staff to achieve?) and then formulate the steps necessary to achieving those goals (better canvassing? working longer hours? better customer service?). How can these steps be explained in terms of clear, achievable tasks – and what is the most logical order for these to be presented to your staff? Important goals and important specific tasks should be given to your team in writing. Every salesperson should be given a detailed written job description outlining all areas of performance and responsibility and setting out clear levels of performance. For further information, see Chapter 4 on Job Descriptions and Chapter 5 on Goal Setting.

Help, advise and support

Always be there to offer help, advice and support to your staff. Never be 'too busy' (but keep an eye on Time Management) and when you offer advice, always ask later to see if your advice was (i) acted upon and (ii) of any use.

As manager, you are in some ways responsible for your staff's personal and emotional happiness as well as their professional success: always be sympathetic, even when you cannot help (in which case are there 'professionals', such as priests, marriage guidance counsellors, housing officers and so on you can refer them to). As staff get used to coming to you with their problems, they will look to you more for leadership in other things. However, never prevent them from having and using their own ideas – you want to be leading a team of people who are confident in their own abilities. Also, beware of staff taking advantage of your support and using their problems to excuse their performance – in this instance, you may express sympathy, but your staff must know where their priorities must lie.

Develop the right relationship

What is the right relationship between manager and staff? To a certain extent this is something you will instinctively *feel*. Here are a few pointers:

O Sales leaders should be familiar enough with their staff to laugh, joke and cajole informally: if you don't have this 'common touch' it will be much harder to motivate your staff and retain their loyalty.

O Sales leaders must never let familiarity prevent them from 'laying down the law' whenever necessary. You might be a salesperson's friend, but if he/she needs to be disciplined, this must come first. Staff will not respect managers who favour their friends.

O Never apologize for your actions. This encourages staff to question your authority. By all means explain the reason for your actions (and be prepared to admit mistakes), but do not allow staff to debate the validity of your decisions. Often you will make decisions for reasons which cannot be revealed in public, and at the end of the day 'because I say so' must be good enough for your staff.

○   Always treat your staff with respect and as equals. Do not manipulate them for your own ends (this is not the same as directing them for the company's benefit). Do not abuse their trusts and confidences. Do not treat poor performers cruelly. Give staff honest appraisals and promises.

For further ideas on this topic, see 'Applying leadership styles' in Chapter 2.

Discipline and reward

Both discipline and reward must be for two reasons only: *performance* and *attitude*. All staff should know this and agree with it.

Rewards should generally be made public. Everyone should be told why the person was rewarded and should know that if they achieve the same things, they will receive the same rewards.

Ideally punishments should be administered in private, but if they become common knowledge (or you think it better for everyone to know), do not apologize for your actions. State your reasons clearly and objectively – and also let everyone know what the person must do to escape further discipline.

For a full discussion of rewards (praise, promotions, prizes, payrises, benefits) and punishments (warnings, goal-settings, reduction of privileges and so on) see Chapter 5.

POSITION WITHIN THE ORGANIZATION

You cannot lead people effectively unless you have sufficient *authority*, *power*, *prestige* and *freedom of action* within your organization, and undertake *direct supervision*.

The key areas in which every sales manager should have responsibility (*authority* and *power*) are:

○   Recruitment and dismissal
○   Pay reviews
○   Promotions
○   Discipline
○   Commission schemes
○   Setting individual performance goals
○   Organizing training
○   Establishing and defining working practices.

Whenever you lead staff, you do so with the tacit implication of either a 'stick' (discipline, no promotion, your displeasure, their own poor performance) or a 'carrot' (promotion, pay review, your goodwill, their improved performance). If you don't control the areas listed above, your ability to offer sticks and carrots is greatly reduced. If your staff do not care about pleasing or displeasing you or do not think your advice will improve their performance, they will not listen to you. Crucially, staff must know that:

○   they were recruited on your say-so,
○   they will progress on your say-so, and
○   they will be dismissed on your say-so.

If you are not responsible for these functions, staff may see the people who are responsible for them as the people they ought to please – not you. If you do not conduct these functions personally, make it clear that the decisions, promotions and so on are based on your recommendations or are in keeping with your views.

Leadership does not only concern power; it also involves *prestige*: the sales manager and the sales department as a whole must be treated with respect by other senior members of your company. If they are not, you have a serious problem: any company which does not understand or value the contribution of the sales department is not a company a salesperson or sales manager should work for (and they probably won't be in business for too long either!). The sales manager must have sufficient prestige to be able to defend the interests of his/her team and department in any 'internal' company disputes.

The other important criterion is *freedom of action*. As sales manager you must be seen as 'master of your own house': you must be free to respond quickly to changing circumstances (either within the sales team or in the market) as you see fit – after all, you are in the best position to judge what will or won't be effective. You should not have to refer every decision 'up the line' for approval: staff will soon sense this and either become demoralized or lose respect for the manager.

Conversely, some managers run the risk of being too 'senior' and consequently too remote. For this reason, always try to keep in touch with 'the sales floor'. Even when senior sales executives or team leaders look after staff on a day-to-day basis, if at all possible retain some direct involvement in supervising all staff. Direct supervision should include: monitoring performance, praising, correcting faults and discussing work with salespeople.

WAYS OF WORKING

Effective management cannot be explained simply in terms of personal qualities, treating others, and organizational position. It must also be understood in the way you put these into practice, namely through time management, organization, appearance and efficiency.

Time management

As a manager your single most valuable personal resource is *your time*. Use it; don't lose it. If you are able to manage and organize your time efficiently, you can get more hours out of the day. You will also be a better manager, and will experience less stress and disorganization. There are many time management systems available on the market, and it is worth investigating them if you find time management a problem. However, the following methods may help:

- **Plan your day the night before.** Before leaving work, review your activities scheduled for the next day and draw up a plan (or at least a list of things to do) while everything is fresh in your mind.
- **Re-plan your work each morning.** The next morning review your plan. This will remind you of what lies ahead. You may also make changes in the light of the new day.
- **Prioritize your work.** Every plan needs the sense of priority. Managers should always prioritize their tasks. Tasks should be prioritized according to the following criteria:

    Deadline: When does this task have to be done? If the task is necessary, but not important, can you change the deadline to suit you?
    Necessity: Does this task have to be done? What would happen if it wasn't?
    Benefits: What benefits will follow from this task? Use this test to judge how important a task is, in conjunction with:
    Drawbacks: What drawbacks will follow from not doing this task?
    Personal commitment: Will someone be let down if I don't do this? Have I given my word to do this?

    Use these criteria to divide your tasks into the following groups:

    Must be done
    Would like to do
    Can wait.

Must be done includes all those tasks which are necessary, have deadlines, have been personally promised, or which entail dire drawbacks or excellent benefits (usually in this order).

Would like to do includes those tasks which are not necessary or urgent but will give benefits or avoid drawbacks. Where there is no obvious order of priority, do them in order of speed and ease.

Can wait is everything else.

Each day aim to do everything which must be done and some of the things which you would like to do. Don't do anything which can wait unless there is really nothing else you can do.

- **Do one thing at a time.** You will work more efficiently and more quickly if you concentrate on one task at a time. This is why interruptions are so fatal. Do not let yourself be distracted by anything less than what is absolutely urgent. Let your staff know that when you are engaged in a task which must be done, they should not interrupt you unless time or money is critical. If customers ring, they can be told you are in a meeting and will ring them back (obvious exceptions are if the customer wants to place an order or has a serious complaint). Everything else can wait until a free period (see below).
- **Structure your day:** Divide your day into blocks, probably an hour each. Decide which task (usually starting with the most important first) you will achieve in which block. The secret to structuring your day is to leave yourself *free time*. Every sales manager will be interrupted throughout the day by problems and queries from salespeople or customers. Allow yourself space to handle these when they will not disturb your main tasks: say 45 minutes free time before lunch and again at four o'clock. Then whenever you are interrupted, tell your staff you will deal with the matter at your next free time. Staff will soon learn to respect this and appreciate it helps you to help them.
- **Act efficiently:** Don't fuss over jobs. Get them done quickly, efficiently, then move on.
- **Always have time for people:** You may be too busy to help a salesperson, but always take time to show you are interested and make a firm promise to come back to them, either during free time or at the end of work.
- **Review your working practices:** Are there any tasks or duties you undertake which are laborious, inessential or time-consuming? Does the effort involved outweigh their benefits? Could these tasks be done by subordinates, without reducing your authority and control? Can you make more use of computerization? If you are expected to perform too many functions within your department, discuss this with your superiors – or else you may find yourself unfairly criticized.

In addition to time management, there are other ways of working which are important.

Organization

A successful sales manager must be well organized. Otherwise you will not get the best out of yourself, your time, and your staff. Conversely, if you are disorganized or untidy, you will lose the respect of your staff (and they too will be disorganized), you will make more mistakes and miss opportunities, you will fail to keep to deadlines and you will lose important information.

Keep records

Record everything that is important: any discussions you have had with staff about their careers or expectations, any rewards or disciplines, any promises. Likewise record all sales and performance figures meticulously: if you don't show you take them seriously, neither will your staff. (This subject is covered more fully in Chapter 9.)

Use records

Base your decisions and actions on records, figures and data. Never guess. Often the solution to a problem lies in the detail, not in a generalization. (Chapter 8 includes treatment of this topic.)

SUMMARY

In this chapter we have examined sales leadership in terms of personal qualities, ways of treating staff, organizational position, and the management of time and personal resources. In Chapter 2 we review ways of putting sales leadership *into practice*.

2

SALES LEADERSHIP IN PRACTICE

In Chapter 1 we examined many of the qualities and working practices which go to make a sales leader. This chapter looks at specific, practical ways of applying this in the workplace. First and foremost, leadership involves people. A leader's success or failure – in fact your whole leadership style – is determined by the ways you and your team interact. Two of the most important elements of this relationship are *motivation* and *rewards and punishment*. These topics are covered in some detail in Chapters 3, 4, 5 and 7. In this chapter we consider the following subjects:

O   Managing by goals
O   Building the sales team
O   Applying leadership styles
O   Managing change
O   Managing difficult staff.

MANAGING BY GOALS

One of the key characteristics of a successful leader is having clear goals, and inspiring the sales team to achieve these goals. It follows that your first concern as sales manager will be to define and understand your goals and to prioritize them accordingly. For most sales managers, although they may have many short-term aims and problems, their performance and organizational goals are defined on a yearly basis, corresponding naturally enough to the sales year.

Your primary goals may well be set by your manager or director, or by the terms of your job description. If you have more than one goal, the relative priority of each one should also be made clear. If they are not, it is probably best consulting with your manager before progressing: it is vital that you both agree which goals you should achieve first, or to which you should devote most of your resources.

Sometimes it will be your responsibility to define your own goals. Even if your 'official' goals are clearly defined, you will still have to decide how to achieve them, and what other personal goals you have. Following is a five-stage method of goal assessment:

1   Where are we now?
2   Where can we go?
3   What lies ahead?
4   How do we get there?
5   How can we measure progress?

WHERE ARE WE NOW?

Start by assessing your own management performance and the performance and status of your sales team. Evaluating your own performance is difficult: it is easy to be overcritical or overindulgent. Instead, refer to the key skills described in Chapter 1, and use them as an initial checklist. Assessing your sales team is described in detail in Chapter 8. Above all, your assessment will probably be concerned with your team's sales performance: how many sales are they making, and with what value? Do you think it is satisfactory, or could it be improved?

WHERE CAN WE GO?

Next you should review the goals which are available to you and, in particular, what improvements you can – or need to – make. Your considerations will give you your primary goals, so take great care in formulating them, and express them in as precise a form as possible. Typical goals would be:

- Increase sales by 10 per cent a year.
- Improve the quality of training, particularly at induction level.

WHAT LIES AHEAD?

Now examine the potential opportunities and difficulties which lie between you and your goals. Critical factors might be a slump in the market, the increase in computerization, easier credit facilities for your customers. How do they affect you? Can they help or hinder you, or do they offer other goals?

HOW DO WE GET THERE?

A detailed plan is required of the means you will employ to achieve your goals. This may include subgoals, and should involve specific tasks which you can communicate to your staff.

HOW CAN WE MEASURE PROGRESS?

For a goal to be meaningful, you have to be able to tell how you are progressing, and if you have achieved it. When your goals are vague, such as 'Improve team morale', they become more difficult to achieve. The solution is to redefine general goals in terms of specifics. For instance, you might define 'Improve team morale' as follows: staff to identify with team goals, to be more punctual, to willingly stay later, to be more enthusiastic about goal-setting, staff resignations to drop by half. This gives you a clearer goal, and a better means of gauging your success in achieving it.

MANAGING BY GOALS – AN EXAMPLE

The following example shows how managing by goals works in practice. Assuming a typical situation where your 'official' goal is to boost annual sales by 10 per cent, typical options would be:

- To improve the motivation of staff.
- To improve their sales ability through training.
- To generate a better source of new leads.
- To implement a tighter system of monitoring performance.
- To get each person to contribute more through individual goal-setting.
- To lose fewer customers.

You will see that, in addition to being a means to an end, each of these approaches is a subgoal in itself.

You might also have other goals, less directly relevant to achieving your official goal, but equally important to the long-term success of the sales team. These might be:

- To introduce a more structured sales department.
- To introduce regular pay reviews and promotions.
- To reduce staff turnover.
- To recruit and train better-quality staff.

(All of the goals listed above are described in detail later in this book or in its companion volume, *Training the Sales Team*.)

In addition, you will probably have personal goals of your own. These are important if you are to continue to find your work stimulating and interesting. These might be:

- To manage my time and energies more effectively.
- To reduce my stress.
- To boost the prestige of the sales department in the company as a whole.
- To present myself as suitable material for promotion.

Once you have arrived at a full list of your goals, subgoals and the primary means of achieving them, prioritize them carefully, probably according to A, B or C categories. Naturally, in the course of a year you can achieve a great deal, so do not be surprised or worried if you have many A priorities. (Only be concerned if they are mutually exclusive!)

Regularly review your list of goals

Assess your goals once a month. Are they still valid and relevant? Are they still achievable? If they are not, you need to redefine them in accordance with what is important and practicable. How are you progressing towards them? Do your proposed means appear to be achieving your desired results, or should you think about initiating new or additional methods?

Get your staff to share your goals

Insofar as is possible and sensible, your staff should know what your goals are and should identify with them. For this reason, present your goals in terms which are attractive to them. For instance, don't say 'This year, I want you all to make 10 per cent more sales' but 'My aim is to help you all do 10 per cent better than last year.' Bear in mind that annual targets may be too vague for your staff to grasp, in which case present your goal in more short-term stages, usually during your sales meetings. (For coverage of this topic, see Chapter 6.) 'This month let's try to increase sales by at least 10 per cent.'

Tell them the positive aspects of how you plan to help them: better training, more free time to solve their problems, better organization, less paperwork.

Ask your staff for questions, suggestions, queries and advice. It may be possible for your staff to prepare annual or quarterly marketing plans for their territories, detailing how each of them intends to develop their customer base, improve their sales and achieve their – and your – goals.

As the year progresses, keep your staff informed on their progress, praise them for being 'on target', and continue to ask for feedback and suggestions.

Can you reinforce the achievement of your annual sales target by rewarding your team with a suitable prize? (This subject is covered in detail in Chapter 7.)

Even though your goals are of the utmost importance, never let your staff feel that this is all you are interested in: they must feel you care about them as *people*, not simply as the means to an end.

BUILDING THE SALES TEAM

WHAT IS A TEAM?

The first question to ask yourself is: 'Is my sales force a sales *team*?' What I mean by 'team' is this: a group of people who may have varying roles but who share a common goal, work towards that goal together, and depend on and help each other to achieve their goal. This common goal, and the unity and organization needed to make the team work, are provided by their leader.

Does your sales force meet this definition of a team? In what ways does it not? Often sales 'teams' are in reality groups of individual salespeople, each responsible for a given sales territory, and each succeeding or failing on their individual merits. There are many good reasons for encouraging your staff to work and think like a team. We will review them briefly below.

WHY YOU SHOULD BUILD YOUR STAFF INTO A TEAM

- In order to achieve group sale targets. Otherwise salespeople will work according to what suits them best: they may even stop working when they achieve their own individual targets.
- To encourage staff to share leads and pass on information.
- So that staff take messages for each other and cover for each other because of sickness, holidays and so on.
- To boost morale: morale is essentially a team-based emotion, most commonly expressed as 'team spirit' or *esprit de corps*.
- To introduce changes: people will be happier to comply if they see that the changes are for the good of the group.
- To reduce poor performance and behaviour: if staff feel accountable to the team as well as to themselves, they will perform more consistently.
- Greater team-loyalty means lower staff turnover, more job satisfaction, a stronger sense of 'belonging', more security, less disruption, and encourages staff to look for praise and recognition within the group.
- Strong 'sense of team' enables you to motivate and problem-solve on the team level (as opposed to one-to-one): this makes your life easier, and your efforts more productive.
- Good team spirit discourages the development of harmful cliques or the emergence of rebellious salespeople.
- The stronger the team, the stronger the need for, and effectiveness of, the leader.

To summarize: to be a team leader, you need a team to lead. If you don't organize a team, then you are abdicating one of the greatest functions and responsibilities of management. The more you can build up your sales force's sense of being a team, the more that team will look to you to lead and help them.

HOW TO BUILD A TEAM

Give your staff common goals and aims

It is probably best to give each salesperson individual targets and pay him/her according to individual performance – this is the only way to get the best out of salespeople. But you can also give your staff group targets and aims. Staff should be told what constitutes good or bad performance for the group as a whole, and they should be encouraged to work towards it. And make it worth their while: can you offer overriding team commission as well as individual commission? Or if this is not feasible, can you at least make sure that your commission structure encourages staff to beat their personal targets and contribute more to the team? (For a full treatment of this subject, see Chapter 7.)

Team goals need not be based on sales or money: they might focus on corporate goals such as a better overall quality of service, fewer customer complaints, a greater number of leads converted, faster turnarounds of new accounts. Or you might define team goals in terms of your competitors: more new business than your closest rival, greater market share in a particular county.

Praise your staff for teamwork

The best way of encouraging teamwork is to praise staff when they pull together, and to praise them in front of the team. In addition, can you take the team out for a drink, or provide a team-based prize, such as a new coffee-maker for the kitchen, or offer a cup/plaque to the salesperson who contributes most to the team each month?

Regular sales meetings

The more you address your sales force as a team and the more you ask them to contribute and share their ideas, the more they will see themselves as a team. (See Chapter 6 for a full treatment of this topic.)

Group competitions

Organize regular prizes and competitions within the team for best sales figures, best canvass figures and so on. (Chapter 7 provides full details.)

Group training and problem-solving

Encourage your staff to talk about their common problems and help them to develop solutions together. The companion volume to this book, *Training the Sales Team*, will show you ways of doing this.

Introduce team structure

Generate more interest in the team by giving staff seniority and responsibility for the performance, training or 'moral support' of others in the group. Alternatively, are there any activities you can allocate (perhaps on a rota basis) to encourage team interdependence, such as opening the morning mail, reading the press for new leads, going to exhibitions?

Handling emotionally-toned issues

You will build and reinforce team values by treating emotionally-toned issues with consideration and tact. Particular issues which should be handled sensitively are: personal tragedies, dismissing or disciplining staff (even unpopular ones), promoting staff (avoiding jealousy).

Your own mood and attitude

As sales manager, your own feelings and mood will dramatically affect the group as a whole. If you are feeling demoralized or bored, this will make itself known to your staff – and produce the same result in them. Assess your presentation: do you convey enthusiasm, optimism and conviction?

SOME MISTAKES TO AVOID

Don't think everyone has to be the same

Teams usually work best (and are most dynamic) when their members are different, varied, with their own styles, approaches, personalities and so on, as long as they are united in a common sense of goals and professionalism. Trying to impose uniformity on such a team will merely demoralize everyone.

Don't do away with individual sales targets and individual commission

Without these incentives you will merely encourage mediocrity – and you will lose your best performers to organizations who do reward achievement.

Don't expect the team to take responsibility for itself

By all means make your team aware of common problems (within reason), and if they can solve these problems themselves, so much the better. But ultimately this is not the team's responsibility: it is always for *you* to provide the leadership and dedication to solve these problems.

APPLYING LEADERSHIP STYLES

There is no one style of leadership which is universally successful. Different situations, different individuals call for different approaches. Recent research has shown that successful managers will apply two, three and even four different leadership styles.

A good way to analyse different leadership styles is in terms of control. At one extreme there is the authoritarian 'take charge' style where the manager will demand total control over the workforce; at the other extreme is the 'laissez-faire' style of the manager who gives staff free rein to set their own goals and organize their work as they see fit.

Any analysis like this is bound to be a little artificial: in some senses the differences between the styles of management are absolute; in others, they are simply a matter of degree. If you find this sort of breakdown too complex, try to focus on the three key differences of approach which this system assumes: total control, team-based consultation, and individual self-starting.

The important principle to understand is that all five approaches are equally valid – there is nothing intrinsically better or worse about being a 'democrat' or a 'dictator' (in terms of management, that is!) – but certain approaches will be more effective in specific situations and you should adapt your behaviour accordingly. A few words of advice might be added here.

Start tough

When taking over a new management task, it is better to start with high standards of discipline which you can then relax, as opposed to being lax and then trying to enforce discipline. Make a full appraisal of your staff, their competence and their attitude before deciding on any course of action.

Never give way to hostility

Meet challenges to your authority head-on, but only if you have to. If you can change the troublemaker's perception and attitude instead, so much the better, but never act in any way which could suggest weakness, cowardice or lack of authority.

Recognize that some staff want to be given direction

Many staff feel most comfortable, and will perform best, if they are told exactly what to do and how to do it. If you fail to do this, you will lose their motivation and their respect.

Always treat your staff with respect

Even if the situation calls for severity.

TABLE 2.1 LEADERSHIP STYLES

Style:	Dictator	Governor	Consultant	Democrat	Servant of the people
Description:	Total control	Full control, but with consideration	Control, with consultation	Sets agenda for discussion	Lets staff control work
Targets:	Imposes as sees fit	Sets with consultation	Sets parameters	Agrees	Allows own targets
Orientation:	Specific tasks	Specific tasks	Overall goals	Overall goals	Personal goals
Responsibility:	Leader	Leader	Leader	Group	Individual
Attitude:	No trust	Some trust	Fair trust	Trust	Total trust
Requires:	Total obedience	Willingness to be guided	Co-operation, participation	Teamwork, participation	Initiative, motivation
Monitoring:	Total	Sets and agrees standards	Periodic focus on end-results	End-results, plus reports on progress	None – may ask for report
Discipline:	Strict punishments for failure to comply	Punishes if overall work not acceptable	Expects compliance, but respects freedom to interpret goals	Only when performance poor or when affects the group	Only in matters which affect group
Effective for:	Junior, inexperienced, hostile, or complacent staff. Crises and emergencies	Mature staff who want direction. Low performers, junior inexperienced	Co-operative, mature, experienced, competent staff	Co-operative, responsible, enthusiastic, team-minded staff	Experienced individualistic staff, highly motivated, keen to make decisions
Inappropriate for:	Experienced, or motivated staff. Tasks requiring teamwork, quality	Individualistic, or mature, competent staff	Inexperienced staff	Fast decisions. Demotivated, or hostile staff. Staff who like leadership	Inexperienced, or hostile, or demotivated staff. Staff who like guidance
Comments:	Fast, ruthless decisions, short-term goals	Restores order. Ensures sense of direction	Works well when things are going well	Needs time, well-informed, responsible staff	Gives scope to self-disciplined high-flyers

MANAGING CHANGE

Change is an integral part of life. Much recent thought on business management portrays managers as the implementors and managers of change. Certainly one of a manager's worst failings is to refuse to recognize change, and to fail to anticipate it or respond to it. Nowhere is this more true than in sales, where your very success or failure will depend on your reading of the market.

HOW TO ANTICIPATE CHANGE

Listen to your staff

Your staff are dealing with hundreds of businesses. They are asking customers about their needs, their plans for the future, and about what the competition are offering. Regularly consult with your staff as part of your sales meetings. If staff tell you of new developments, take time to assess them seriously: will this impact on your business – and how? Does this represent new opportunities for growth – or less?

Participate in trade organizations

Many sales managers see trade associations as a waste of valuable time. So they can be. But they are one of the few sources of information open to you. I have known sales managers who were blaming the market for poor performance when competitors were increasing sales by 50 per cent.

Read, read, read

Everything topical – newspapers, magazines, as well as trade press and journals. The fact that you are reading this book shows you are interested in acquiring new information.

Give yourself time

Set yourself an hour once a month for anticipating change. Review any information you have received: what does it tell you? Can you foresee any developments? Should you be considering new initiatives? The more you do this, the more effective your attempts will become.

Remember that people change as well

Review your staff constantly. How are they progressing? Are any of them ready for new responsibilities or challenges?

IMPLEMENTING CHANGE

Change frightens and disturbs people. The present suddenly becomes an uncertain place. You can minimize this in the following ways:

- Discuss change: If you have identified the need for change, discuss the options in your sales meetings (for full details see Chapter 6, 'Implementing change'). Encourage your staff to contribute their ideas and so *feel part of* the change.
- Explain change: Tell people why change is necessary – and explain how it benefits *them*.
- Signpost change: Don't just spring surprises on people. Let your staff know what is happening – and when.
- Train for change: Give staff adequate training in new tasks.
- Praise: Praise staff for adapting to new situations. Do not criticize.
- Review change: Let your staff know that no change is irreversible. Review changes. Have they achieved your aims? Are there unforeseen advantages or disadvantages? Should adjustments be made?
- Use change to stimulate: Sometimes 'a change *is* as good as a rest'. Simply by changing things around, you can create an impression of dynamism. If you work in an office-based environment which has become stale, it can be a good idea to move everyone's desks. This refreshes people's outlooks and stops cliques developing. These sorts of changes should *not* be signposted: their unpredictability and disruptive quality is what helps them revive a jaded workforce.

MANAGING DIFFICULT STAFF

The more you implement the styles and approaches advocated in this book, the less you should find that you encounter salespeople who are deliberately 'difficult'. Coping with 'difficult' people is part of every sales manager's job, no matter how 'good' a leader you are. This subject is covered in general in the chapters on motivating your staff (Chapters 3 and 4) and specifically in 'Managing Difficult Staff' (Chapter 14).

SUMMARY

In this chapter we have reviewed various practical means and styles of applying leadership to the sales team. Almost all of these depend on the type of people you are leading. In the next chapter, therefore, we explore one of the most important aspects of sales leadership, namely understanding and motivating the people who make up your team.

3

MOTIVATION

The contents of this chapter are as follows:

- An introduction to motivation
- Understanding motivation through needs
- A simple theory of needs
- Analysing your staff's needs
- Appealing to your staff's needs
- The theory of roles
- Appendix – Theories of motivation.

AN INTRODUCTION TO MOTIVATION

More has probably been written about motivation than any other aspect of management. And with good reason, for the ability to motivate staff is the essential ingredient of all good management. In sales, with its emphasis on getting individuals to achieve personal and group targets, motivation is particularly important. Consequently a sales manager who cannot motivate his or her staff to perform, will be judged to fail in the primary task.

There are some fundamental aspects of human motivation:

1. **Motivation comes through good leadership.** All of the great leaders in business, politics and history have been superb motivators *because* they were great leaders, not the other way around. If you can capture your staff's imagination and excitement, they will be motivated. And if you lose their respect, you will lose their motivation.

2. **There is no one single theory of human motivation.** As we shall see, there are as many good theories of motivation as there are good psychologists. This doesn't mean that these theories cannot give us profound insights into human nature, but we shouldn't be afraid of drawing our own conclusions and acting on them. The best place to learn about the motivation of your sales force is by listening to them and understanding them *as people*. There is a review of the main theories of human motivation in the Appendix at the end of this chapter (see pages 30–2).

3. **Motivation is ultimately to do with the self.** Motivation is never concerned with telling people to do what you want. It involves instead getting people to want the same thing as you, so they see your task as *their* task. This is vital in a profession like sales where everything depends not on what you do, but on how you do it.

4   **Motivation comes from your own belief and enthusiasm.** Your staff will expect you to set the tone of their work: if you believe in your goals, your company and your products, so will they. If you do not, you will never be able to motivate them.

MOTIVATION COMES THROUGH GOOD LEADERSHIP

The first point in the list is probably the most important. If you can become a good leader, and apply the techniques and attitudes outlined in Chapters 1 and 2, you will find that motivation comes easy: *people want to work for a good leader*. The contents of this chapter should be understood in the context of successful team leadership.

UNDERSTANDING MOTIVATION THROUGH NEEDS

Knowing how to motivate your staff is like knowing how to sell. In sales, you appeal to the customers' needs to induce them to want your product. In motivation, you appeal to your staff's needs and ambitions to influence them to want to do what you're asking them to do. In other words, you show them how it will personally *benefit* them. Sometimes the benefits will be real and positive, such as praise, greater success, more commission, or promotion. Sometimes the benefits will lie in the absence of hardship, such as no failure, no loss of earnings, no displeasure from management. Exactly how you apply the carrots and sticks of motivation must depend on your judgement, your situation and the people you are leading.

Let's start by examining people's needs. This will help us be aware of the different ways in which different people can be motivated.

A SIMPLE THEORY OF NEEDS

At the end of this chapter, there is a survey of the most commonly held theories of motivation. They make fascinating reading, and can offer useful insights. As you shall see, all theories have weaknesses as well as strengths and need to be interpreted with a pinch of common sense.

The 'theory' that follows isn't really a theory at all. Rather it is an exercise to help you become aware of the range of different needs which affect human actions. It is also the most helpful and practical method I have come across.

Human beings have two types of needs. The first type is to do solely with physical survival at its most basic. They are the need for food, water, oxygen, warmth and so on. Unless you are operating on the surface of the Moon, these needs are not particularly relevant to us. What does concern us is the second type of need: the *emotional* and *psychological* needs people have, which account for almost all human actions. These are listed below. Some psychologists try to put these needs in some order of priority, but this is not of much practical help to us, as what one person regards as important, another may not.

- Pride
- Peer group pressure
- Interest/curiosity
- Care for loved ones
- Need for security
- Lust
- Loyalty
- Habit
- Greed

- Power
- Competitive spirit
- Desire to be liked
- Desire to be helpful
- Desire for praise or recognition
- Excitement
- Ease
- Comfort
- Fear
- Boredom
- Religious, political or moral conviction
- Peace of mind.

How many more can you think of? The list can be as long as you want to make it – our sole aim is to increase our awareness of the many different reasons *why* people act, so that almost any human action can be explained by referring to one, or a combination, of these motivations.

Notice that none of these motivators is a physical object, such as 'money' or 'better salary' or 'a holiday in Spain'. **Objects do not motivate people:** people want objects for the *benefits* they bring, and they want benefits because of what they *need*.

Using 'the carrot'

It follows that we can motivate our staff by offering them things in terms of their personal needs. Of course, different people will often want the same thing, but for different reasons. To illustrate this, let's examine one typical 'carrot' which managers offer their staff – a better salary. Why might people want to earn more money? There are many obvious, practical answers, but look at the range of reasons which people may have, depending on which needs motivate them the most:

- Pride: The employee equates what he/she earns with their worth as a person.
- Peer group pressure: The employee wants more money because his/her friends have just had a payrise.
- Greed: The employee just loves money!
- Power: The employee feels more powerful and has more control over his/her living conditions.
- Comfort: The employee loves to eat out and buy luxuries.
- Care for loved ones: The employee wants to treat his/her children to a holiday.
- Peace of mind: The employee does not want to worry about cash flow.

I could continue. But the point to be learned from this example is that instead of relying on money to keep our staff enthusiastic and committed, we should be motivating our staff in other ways. For instance:

- Pride: This employee might be better motivated if he/she is offered a new job title, or is given public recognition for their achievements.
- Peer group pressure: Maybe the employee needs to be told how essential he/she is to the team, or will be motivated by a company party.
- Greed: Maybe a bonus, or a new commission incentive, will produce more of a return than a simple payrise.
- Power: A promotion, or some sort of responsibility or administrative function, may satisfy this need and keep your employee motivated.
- Comfort: What about dining or clothes allowances – say £20 a month, a lot less than a £500 a year payrise?
- Care for loved ones: How else can we tap into this? Maybe through more interest in the employee's family, or a medical insurance scheme, or by promising long-term prospects.

○	Peace of mind: Give employees other sources of security: offer praise, say what they need to do to make their position secure. Employees may actually become *demotivated* if they are made to feel unduly insecure.

Offering people a payrise is a simple, effective and legitimate management 'carrot'. But payrises are only truly effective if we also understand how to motivate our staff on a personal basis. Used on their own, payrises only bring short-term benefits, and the original causes of demotivation, unless treated, will reassert themselves.

Using 'the stick'

Of course, motivation is not simply a matter of pandering to employees' needs or wants. Motivators can also be used to discipline your staff. For instance, an employee who is motivated by pride may work harder to avoid the embarrassment of failing. Just as offering a promotion may motivate someone, so may telling them they cannot be promoted unless their performance improves (for treatment of this, see Chapter 5 on 'Goal-setting'). People who want security may be inspired to work by the fear of *in*security. They may also fail to respond positively to a new initiative which appears to threaten them.

One of the golden rules of motivation is: *you can't push on a piece of string* – in other words, you cannot force needs, only work with them. And if you do use 'sticks' to motivate staff, you must do so constructively: by giving them targets to achieve which *will* benefit them.

ANALYSING YOUR STAFF'S NEEDS

A useful exercise at this stage is to try to analyse each of your staff's motivations in the light of what we have been discussing. Draw up a chart like the one in Figure 3.1 (or make a photocopy of it) and see if you can rate the strength of each motivation in your staff on a scale of 1 to 5.

You will probably find that by attempting this exercise you will gain valuable insights into:

○	yourself and how you view the world,
○	your staff, and
○	how little you really know, and how much you take for granted, about your staff.

Once you have done this, bear the results in mind. Then put them aside and come back to them a month later. Do you still agree with your analysis? Were you wrong? Or have your staff changed? Use this test as a basis for getting to know your staff better. As your understanding of your staff deepens, you can start to make notes on their motivations and how they develop as part of their reviews.

A WORD OF WARNING

Although this exercise can give us useful insights, we must try not to play the amateur psychologist. Beware of pigeon-holing staff in ways which bear no relationship to reality, such as 'Bill's prime motivation is his pride, Mary just wants to fit in, Gary wants enough money to buy a sports car', and so on. Human beings are just too complex, and they change too dramatically! If you want a full and detailed analysis of your staff's personalities, a professional psychometric testing consultancy can provide computerized assessments for as little as £25 per person – and the results can be invaluable.

FIGURE 3.1   STAFF MOTIVATION QUESTIONNAIRE

NAME OF PERSON:..

	1	2	3	4	5
Pride					
Peer group pressure					
Interest					
Loved ones					
Security					
Loyalty					
Habit					
Greed					
Power					
Competitive spirit					
To be liked					
To be helpful					
Praise					
Excitement					
Ease					
Comfort					
Fear					
Boredom					
Conviction					
Peace of mind					

APPEALING TO YOUR STAFF'S NEEDS

We have looked at our list of human motivations – but how can we use it in our everyday work? This section offers some suggestions. Remember that not all people are motivated by all needs.

Pride

Most salespeople are motivated by pride to some extent. If nothing else you must encourage them to take pride in their work. Make your staff feel their effort is important, and that you value their skills. Use phrases such as 'set the right example', 'I can count on you', 'the others will take their lead from you'. However, don't overflatter: feel free to use such criticisms as 'you of all people shouldn't . . .', 'I want to talk to you before your behaviour becomes a problem', and so on. Don't belittle the pride-motivated person – it can lead to resentment, or even resignation.

Peer group pressure

The person motivated by peer group pressure does not want to let the side down, be the odd one out, or the lowest performer: use phrases like 'the team are counting on you', 'we can all do this together'. He/she is unlikely to be the one to initiate action.

Interest

Involve this person in problem-solving. Ask for their ideas. Leave tasks open-ended. Offer opportunities to gain product knowledge or training.

Security

Show that by doing what you are asking, the person will become more secure, their lives easier, their work more predictable. Someone with a great need for security will particularly dislike any system which exposes him/her to failure or managerial scrutiny. Provide routines, structure. Regularly reassure staff that they are doing well.

Loyalty

Encourage and reward with praise and recognition. Never take people for granted. Be loyal to your staff. People often leave jobs because they don't feel their loyalty was repaid by their manager.

Habit

Most of us do most things for no better reason than habit. Habit also makes us reluctant to change. Overcome habit by managing change sensitively (see Chapter 2 for a full treatment of this topic). Encourage good habits by establishing routines for your staff.

Greed

Show how your advice, encouragement and so on will help your staff earn more money. You must make sure your commission systems stimulate a certain element of greed in everyone. Greed is good in sales. It is one of the motivators which keeps people wanting more. Praise high-earners and never make them feel 'guilty'. Only beware: don't let people cut corners for quick results or give up if results (and commission) are slow in coming. Never insult someone by assuming that their only interest is money.

Power

Offer people some power over their environment, or show how they can achieve power if they are successful. By power I mean control over their sales territory, a position of team-leading or maybe rota-monitoring, the personal freedom that comes with higher earnings – or the power which comes from getting a customer to say 'Yes'.

Competitive spirit

Encourage competition with praise and prizes. Focus and channel competitive natures by showing them *where* they can compete successfully. For instance: 'you could be our best telecanvasser'; 'you could have the best-kept records in the team'; 'it's between you and Pete for the best figures this afternoon'. Don't make work too competitive: people can resent having to compete against each other pointlessly; others can shy away from competitions. People only want to compete for things which they might win, and are worth winning.

Desire to be liked

Wanting to be liked is a very common emotion. Sometimes it can be counter-productive in sales as it can make staff reluctant to 'upset' their customers by pushing for business. It does have its positive side: people will want to please you and want to be good team-members.

Desire to be helpful

If someone is keen to help, harness this energy: can the person induct trainees, or collect sales figures for you? Present comments in such language as 'could you help me with this?'; 'I don't find your current attitude very helpful'; 'what ideas do you have...?'

Desire for praise or recognition

Be keen to bestow praise – whenever it is deserved. Never praise indiscriminately – always explain why you are praising, both to reinforce the good performance, and to show sincerity. Whenever you praise, pause for a second to let them enjoy your praise. Establish eye-contact; smile warmly. Never praise grudgingly. Praise staff in front of managers and team-members.

Excitement

Make sales exciting. Be fun and dynamic *yourself*. Don't always do the predictable. Encourage spontaneity.

Ease

Most people prefer the easy option. Harness this as best you can: make it easy for staff to do things 'by the book'; introduce changes smoothly. Beware of short cuts!

Fear

Use fear to motivate if necessary but never abuse it. Employees have a right to be treated with respect and fairness. Managers often use fear needlessly or because they themselves are afraid to confront the real problem: sometimes it is easier to threaten to sack a poor performer than to be honest and tell him/her the reasons for their poor performance.

Sometimes fear *is* the only thing which will focus a salesperson's mind. But give this fear a purpose – set the person clear precise goals which are *achievable*. And when they are achieved, give praise. Fear is abused when you threaten someone for a minor failing, or when you make threats you cannot carry out. For full coverage of this topic, see Chapter 5 on 'Discipline'.

THE THEORY OF ROLES

Another way of understanding your team is in terms of the roles each team-member adopts. This is based on the premise that people within groups tend to act in certain ways and take on certain responsibilities. Over a period of time, everyone in the group will be expected to behave according to their own role. These roles are quite familiar to psychologists and students of group behaviour. Of course, problems with this theory start as soon as you try to define what – and how many – roles exist within a team. Here are some of the more common:

- The Innovator
- The Critic
- The Loner
- The Guardian of the Norms
- The Joker
- The Team Player
- The Weakling
- The Problem Child
- The Helper
- The Bully
- The Sergeant-Major
- The Rebel Leader.

Don't be alarmed by the colourful names! They are explained in more detail below.

The Innovator

The member of the team who likes to have new ideas. He or she can be helpful, or very disruptive, especially if the person refuses to do things by the book. Beware of dismissing their ideas out of hand – this will lead to resentment, or will make you look weak. Often a good way of neutralizing rogue ideas is to have them discussed in sales meetings. Are there harmless or productive ways for this individualism to express itself?

The Critic

Every team needs someone they can trust to evaluate new ideas and test them to destruction. If you're lucky (or skilful) the Critic will spend their time neutralizing ideas proposed by the Innovator. Never be too worried by the Critic – staff will dislike someone who is needlessly critical.

The Loner

Loners don't like going with the herd. Some people are happiest working by themselves, and sometimes the Loner can even help the rest of the team pull together. However, don't leave Loners to their own devices: Loners need a team to be outside of, and can become demotivated if left out.

The Guardian of the Norms

Guardians have one of the most important roles in the team. Their function is to act as authorities on the established way of doing things, group customs and procedures, rather like 'village elders'. Sometimes the manager performs this role (among others), sometimes it is the role of a long-standing and methodical salesperson. Guardians can set standards, but they can also become opponents of change. In times of change, you should try to enlist (or neutralize) the opinion of the Guardian.

The Joker

Every team needs someone who will raise a laugh and relieve tension. Don't worry about Jokers unless they become 'Playboys' who never do any work.

The Team Player

This role is the one taken by someone who is happiest when conforming to the team's expectations and will respond well to any call for 'team effort'. However, don't assume that the Team Player is necessarily any more motivated than, say, the Loner.

The Weakling

The person who struggles to keep up with the rest. Sometimes this is due to genuine weaknesses. Often it is because the person has a 'mental block': you may need to show them they *can* succeed.

The Problem Child

Often motivated by a desire for attention, the Problem Child may deliberately fail to do some simple task, or may be deliberately unruly so that termination may seem the only solution. Do bear in mind that sometimes the Problem Child is a popular team-member and can fulfil the same role as the Joker, acting as a catalyst or source of inspiration. Dismissing such a person, even if justifiable, can lead to resentment. Sometimes it is enough to simply threaten dismissal. Or perhaps you can satisfy their need for attention in another way. Some teams (and some companies) create their own Problem Children – try to determine the root causes before jumping to any conclusions.

The Helper

Sometimes invaluable – the person who takes it upon themselves to welcome new team-members, explain techniques, let you know of any problems. Sometimes they are extremely disruptive, for exactly the same reasons, and can make mountains out of molehills, or can 'help' team-mates adopt bad habits. They can also use their time spent 'helping' as an excuse for their own poor performance.

The Bully

Someone who delights in picking on other team-members or making jokes at their expense. Reasons for this may be insecurity, fear of failure, pride, or just plain old-fashioned aggression. Interestingly enough, many successful salespeople seem to enjoy playing the Bully. You have to decide what is acceptable and what is unacceptable. Never let a Bully bully you. Meet his/her threats calmly, logically and forcefully.

The Sergeant-Major

Identifying a Sergeant-Major can make a valuable contribution. Some people naturally enjoy seeing a team 'pulling together' and will automatically take responsibility for maintaining standards, keeping a watchful eye and so on. If you have a Sergeant-Major in your team, put him/her to good use. Otherwise they may turn into Rebel Leaders.

The Rebel Leader

Every manager's nightmare is the popular team-member who becomes the team's unofficial spokesperson. If this happens, read the chapters on 'Troubleshooting' and 'Managing Difficult Staff'. Note that trying to remove a Rebel Leader by threatening dismissal will usually create more problems than it solves – although it is a legitimate weapon in your arsenal. Often Rebel Leaders arise because of genuine grievances or problems that need addressing – and this should be your first priority. It is probably better not to consult with the Rebel Leader on a one-to-one basis as this may only enhance his/her position (although disciplining in private is a good idea).

A better way is to lead a discussion group and get straight to the heart of the problem: once you show you are keen to devise a solution you have drawn the Rebel Leader's teeth. Devise an alternative which will enable you to regain the initiative. Sometimes Rebel Leaders are merely excusing their own poor performance or their dissatisfaction with their position, in which case they should be set strict performance-related targets to 'make or break' them.

APPLYING THE THEORY

How do you consider the Theory of Roles? I find it helpful because almost every team does seem to create these characters. For instance, if a team's Problem Child leaves, very often another team-member will take on that role. Its weakness is that very often one person can fulfil a variety of roles (a person might be Joker, Problem Child, Rebel Leader all rolled into one).

If you do accept this theory, you may also accept the following conclusions:

O   If I have a problem with a team-member, the problem may lie elsewhere in the team, or in my management of it.

O   Although I can try to channel behaviour, I must recognize I may never be able to eradicate certain roles within my team unless I change my own behaviour. For example, I might remove the need for there to be a Helper if I am myself more helpful and approachable.

O   It is wrong to think about team-members just as individuals. If I want to motivate them I must first of all motivate the whole team.

You may find it helpful to assess your team and see if anyone fits into the roles listed above. Are there other roles we haven't listed? But beware of pigeon-holing!

SUMMARY

I hope this chapter has provided some new approaches to understanding your staff and how to motivate them, to help them work harder, sell more, and be happier. If you are interested in exploring the subject further, have a look at the Appendix which examines the main popular theories.

In Chapters 4, 5, 6 and 7 we investigate ways in which you can encourage and reinforce your staff's motivation through the use of company organization, discipline, goal-setting, commission schemes and competitions.

APPENDIX – THEORIES OF MOTIVATION

What follows is a summary of the theories of motivation widely accepted by psychologists. Each theory provides you with an insight into human behaviour, and may give you additional ideas for motivating and understanding your staff.

MASLOW'S NEED THEORY

Maslow's need theory states that needs exist in an ascending 'hierarchy': our first needs are concerned with survival, and once these are satisfied, other, more developed, needs become apparent, such as safety needs, then social needs, and so on. This hierarchy can be set out as follows:

1. PHYSIOLOGICAL NEEDS
2. SAFETY NEEDS
3. SOCIAL NEEDS
4. ESTEEM NEEDS
5. SELF-ACTUALIZATION NEEDS.

This means that a trainee salesperson will be initially motivated by the need for a basic income to provide the necessities of food, housing, clothes and transport. Once he/she has satisfied those needs, he or she will begin to have safety needs, in other words, wanting job security, a safe place to live and so on. Once these needs are satisfied, he or she will have social needs, which are met through friendship, acceptance in the workplace and so on. After these come esteem needs – praise, recognition, positions of status – and finally self-actualization needs – the desire to be in control of one's destiny, working conditions, achieve self-fulfilment.

If Maslow's theory is correct, the sales manager can keep a salesperson motivated by responding to these needs one after the other, as his career progresses:

Needs:	*Sales Manager to provide:*
Physiological needs –	Adequate basic salary/working conditions
Safety needs –	Security, no threats, safe, healthy environment, medical insurance
Social needs –	Friendly team, social life
Esteem needs –	Praise, promotion, respect
Self-actualization needs –	Responsibility, freedom to make own decisions.

This theory has some obvious flaws: very few people experience needs in this neat, logical order. For instance, many people would rate social needs as more important than many safety needs (except for matters of life and death!) or would look not to their sales manager but to the government for their real safety. Some people – artists are a good example – would put their self-actualization needs before all others. However, this theory does express a valuable truth: as people progress in their careers, they come to expect more from their work and their life. If you cannot meet these expectations, they will either become disillusioned, or go elsewhere.

HERZBERG'S MOTIVATOR–HYGIENE THEORY

Herzberg's theory is well-respected, and for good reason. Herzberg recognizes that the factors which affect motivation can be divided into two groups. One he calls *motivators*, the other *hygiene factors*.

Motivators provide staff with positive motivation to do something. They include achievement, praise, opportunity for growth, job satisfaction, interest. If you do not offer your staff these motivators, they will not be motivated. Hygiene factors, on the other hand, do not in themselves motivate: they provide the right *environment* for staff to be motivated. They include adequate pay, working environment, administrative back-up, company policy, atmosphere. If hygiene factors are non-existent, it will be very difficult to motivate your team no matter what motivators you use.

Herzberg's theory helps us make sense of how to motivate people and keep them motivated. It also shows us how such intangible things as poor office decorations or the wretched state of the company canteen can gradually *de*motivate people.

Herzberg's theory was developed with reference to workers *in general*: it is unable to offer an adequate explanation for the importance of money to a *salesperson*. Many of the best salespeople do not care about their working environment, or company benefits, if they have the opportunity to make good money. Unless you can offer salespeople that, you will never motivate them.

EXPECTANCY THEORY

People are motivated, according to this theory, to work towards a goal in proportion to their expectancy of success – and whether they think the rewards will be worth the effort. In other words, people won't work towards goals which are too hard, or not worth achieving. To make your staff more motivated, so the theory goes, either make their goals more achievable, or more desirable, or both.

There is certainly something to be learned here, especially when devising competitions, prizes or commission scales. What we must always remember, though, is that goals are only desirable if people already have needs: if your salespeople don't *need* to be successful, or don't *need* to earn more money, or are not motivated by praise or criticism, their expectancy is irrelevant.

ACHIEVEMENT THEORY

This theory divides the world's population into two groups: *Achievement-orientated* people and *Affiliative* people.

Achievement-orientated people are motivated by the desire to achieve goals, become high achievers, take on responsibility and so on. They derive more satisfaction from success and more frustration from failure. Because of this, they can take criticism more negatively, and can abandon a course of action, or a job, if they think they are not going to succeed.

Affiliative people are happier working as part of a team. They are more concerned about peer group acceptance and are more likely to help other people.

This theory helps the sales manager to identify and understand high achievers in the team. For them to flourish, high achievers need more feedback (especially about specific tasks), more encouragement, regular praise, more freedom to work on their own, and less criticism.

As theories go, the achievement theory is wildly improbable. The theory takes one aspect of human motivation – achievement – and turns it into a general rule of behaviour. Some people try to achieve tasks in different ways; some respond to criticism in different ways; some high achievers are loners, it is true, but very many are happiest when working in a team.

ATTRIBUTION THEORY

According to the attribution theory, people are motivated to find out why they are successful or unsuccessful in their work. They will attribute their success or failure to such causes as hard work, good fortune, skill, sales training and so on. As one would expect, salespeople will then be motivated to continue to do those things which help them be successful.

Obviously there is some truth in this: often salespeople fail to do their canvassing because they 'don't see the point' or they will use certain sales techniques continuously because they believe they work (even if they don't!). And similarly, a good sales manager will always try to show *why* staff should perform tasks and what the *benefit* will be to them. Nevertheless, the theory does have its limitations: is this the only reason why people do things? How does this account for their other needs?

CONCLUSION

All of the theories reviewed here give valuable insights into human motivation and what people want from their work. All suggest constructive approaches to management and can help managers become more aware of their role and responsibility as team motivator. The fact that there are so many theories demonstrates the need for common sense and sensitivity in these matters.

4

PUTTING MOTIVATION TO WORK

❖

MOTIVATING THROUGH ORGANIZATION

In the last chapter we reviewed ways of understanding and motivating your staff on a personal basis. In this and the following chapters we will see how you can use the actual *management* and *organization* of the sales team to motivate your staff and boost performance. Establishing the right, motivational organization is essential if you are to create a happy, efficient and hardworking sales team. It reinforces the personal motivation and leadership provided by the sales manager, and helps you avoid some of the pitfalls of being the only person responsible for praise, criticism and motivation. Specific benefits of sales-force organization are:

- Good organization enhances the authority and prestige of the manager.
- Organization gives everyone a clear sense of direction and accountability.
- Organization improves efficiency, time management and professionalism.
- Organization encourages good performance, teamwork and morale.
- Without effective organization, morale can plummet if the sales manager is sick, absent or off-form.
- Objective standards are easier to enforce and enable you to praise and criticize fairly.
- Organization enables you to establish an effective management structure.

There are many ways you can use the organization of your sales team to improve and maintain motivation and efficiency. This chapter will examine the following subjects in detail:

- Clear duties, responsibilities and aims
- The job description
- The sales manual
- Clear expectations, standards and grounds for success
- Daily working structure
- Monitoring performance.

In Chapter 5 we survey:

- Constructive goal-setting
- Reviews
- Handling complaints and grievances
- Discipline
- Promotions.

In Chapter 6 we cover:

- Communicating with your staff
- Managing the sales meeting.

In Chapter 7 we review:

- Sales commission schemes
- Prizes and competitions.

CLEAR DUTIES, RESPONSIBILITIES AND AIMS

For people to work hard and effectively they need to be given a clear explanation of what they must do. Without a sense of purpose, and without clear standards to aim at, people quickly become demotivated or adopt personal standards and goals which may have nothing to do with your team objectives. You can solve this in the following ways:

- by the use of clear job descriptions and the sales manual, and
- by establishing clear expectations, standards and grounds for success.

These approaches are considered in the rest of this chapter.

THE JOB DESCRIPTION

Along with the sales manual, the job description has the potential to be the most important motivational document in your organization. It is also, as we shall see in Chapter 11, necessary for recruitment and staff selection purposes. The job description should be shown to candidates at interview stage and should become the blueprint for their training and career progression. It will explain to your staff what they should be doing, and where their responsibilities and priorities lie.

When you are drawing up a salesperson's job description (or reviewing your current one), take nothing for granted. Assume that your staff have never worked in sales before and need to have everything explained and correctly prioritized. Following is a list of all the functions which you will probably need to include.

PURPOSE

Start by stating the primary purpose of the salesperson's work. In almost all cases this is making sales and generating revenue. It may also include building long-term relationships with customers or providing lasting solutions to customers' problems.

CUSTOMER SERVICE

Servicing established customers

Lay out clearly how the salesperson is to do this: for example, through phone-calls, meetings, mailshots. Emphasize the importance of not losing current accounts.

Handling all complaints satisfactorily

Explain the importance of this, and your company's preferred procedure. For ideas about handling complaints, see Chapter 10.

Maintain customer goodwill and loyalty

Part of your salesperson's work of building long-term relationships should include maintaining customer goodwill and loyalty, solving problems, offering constructive advice and so on.

Territory management

Cover all customers regularly (set time-scale) and efficiently.

SALES INITIATIVE

Main purpose

Emphasize that the salesperson's primary purpose is to sell the services of your company, and that their success in this will significantly determine their success in the job as a whole.

Winning new accounts

Stress the importance of new accounts, and explain the steps required: cold calling, visits, presentations and so on.

Overcoming objections/closing sales

The salesperson should try to overcome all objections constructively and try to close sales whenever possible.

Reporting all sales

Salespeople should report all sales, potential sales, and problems to the sales manager immediately.

ADMINISTRATION AND EXECUTIVE RESPONSIBILITIES

Attitude and morale

Salespeople should have a positive, enthusiastic attitude and are responsible for contributing to the morale of the team.

Appearance, presentation, behaviour

Set clear standards.

Administration

The administrative practices, forms, and processes which must be followed should be set out clearly.

Records

State what information the salesperson must record (see Chapter 9 for details).

Reports

List what weekly, or monthly, reports salespeople must prepare, and what information they should report to the sales manager each day. (Chapter 9 covers these topics.)

Sales meetings

Define the salesperson's responsibility to attend and contribute to sales meetings (out of office hours if need be).

Training

Staff must try to improve their sales skills and are to attend training sessions as directed by the sales manager.

ORGANIZATION AND STRUCTURE

Reporting structure

Define who the salesperson reports to (and is accountable to), and the management structure of the sales team.

Reviews

Give times or frequency of reviews, identify who is responsible for reviews (the sales manager), and state the criteria on which promotion or payrises are based (for example, sales figures, hard work).

Goal-setting

Salespeople must contribute to regular goal-settings with the sales manager and must abide by the goals. (For full treatment of this topic, see Chapter 5.)

Sales targets

Salespeople must achieve sales targets as defined by the manager. Failure to do this may result in dismissal.

Sales commission

The job description should include full details of the commission structure, its conditions and so on.

Discipline

The job description should indicate the main grounds for discipline and possible dismissal. These will usually be failure to achieve sales targets and gross insubordination, but they may include failure to report damage to company vehicles, falsifying expense claims, and unprofessional conduct with customers.

THE SALES MANUAL

In addition to the job description, every sales team should have a sales manual. It is hard to overpraise the benefits of a well-presented informative manual. They can be summarized as follows:

- Professionalism: An organized, thorough manual shows the importance of the sales function within your organization.
- Clarity: The sales manual clearly defines the goals, standards and methods of working which are important to your organization.
- Quality: You will not receive high standards from your staff unless you clearly state these standards (and present them suitably).
- Reinforcement: Your manual will reinforce your sales training, and act as a reference book for your courses.
- Encouragement: A good enthusiastic manual will encourage your staff to develop their skills for themselves. Staff should be encouraged to read the manual time and time again.
- Prestige: A well-written and well-presented manual speaks volumes for the prestige of your organization. Likewise, a poorly-worded and badly produced effort will give your new recruits a sinking feeling.

The sales manual should be the bedrock of your staff's performance, sales skills and training programme, setting standards, describing sales techniques and giving your staff every opportunity to develop and hone their skills.

The sales manual should contain the following:

- A definition of the company's business aims and the salesperson's part in fulfilling these.
- A brief history of the company, its products and philosophy.
- A complete salesperson's job description (see preceding section).
- A glossary of all technical jargon.
- How to sell – a complete guide to the company's preferred method of selling.
- Typical problems and objections, and how to overcome them.
- A summary of all administrative and organizational practices.
- A complete product/service guide (where applicable).

Producing a manual like this will take time and effort, but the long-term benefits (and the improvement in sales training) are well worthwhile. Once you have produced a sales manual you will need to review it regularly to ensure it is kept up-to-date and relevant.

CLEAR EXPECTATIONS, STANDARDS AND GROUNDS FOR SUCCESS

If the job description defines *what* your staff should do, you must now define *how much*. Staff must be given objective standards of what is good performance and what is unacceptable. This makes your praise or criticism seem fairer, and stops staff deluding themselves on the one hand or worrying unduly on the other. Typically, the standards you set would be something like this:

- Start work no later than 9.00 am; finish no earlier than 5.30 pm.
- Telephone minimum 40 clients a day.
- Arrange at least two appointments a day.
- Generate at least eight prospects a month.
- Generate sales of at least £5 000 a month (this to be your main priority).
- Success or failure to be determined by monthly sales figures and professional, enthusiastic attitude to company and work.

You might include these figures in your job description. Or you might wish to keep them separate to allow for differences in the sales force, or to make them easier to adapt to changes in the market. If you adopt regular goal-settings with your staff (see Chapter 5), they will supersede these standards.

Note how both the job description and these standards give you the means to discipline your staff as well as reward them. This is important, since it makes the need for such discipline far less likely – *provided your standards are realistic.*

DAILY WORKING STRUCTURE

If your staff are mainly office-based, do they have a set working structure for each day? If not, they could almost certainly benefit from one. If they do, it pays to review it to make sure it is as efficient – and motivational – as possible.

A set working structure is an agreed way for the salespeople to plan and run their work, so that they perform certain tasks at set times of the day. There are many good reasons for this:

- If everyone works together, it is easier to create a 'buzz' within the office and encourage team spirit.

○ By having a pattern to the day, you can help people to manage their time more effectively, whereas, if they are left to their own devices, they may get their priorities wrong.

○ It is easier to monitor performance if you know what everyone is supposed to be doing at any moment of the day.

A typical working structure for an office-based sales team might be as follows:

1. Everyone to have finished any outstanding paperwork by 9.15.
2. 9.15 to 11.30, canvassing – no responding to mail or writing sales proposals except with manager's permission.
3. 11.30 to 1.00, either more canvassing, or writing proposals, if necessary, or responding to mail, or researching leads.
4. 1.00 to 2.00 – lunch.
5. 2.00 to 3.00 – replying to messages that came in that morning and chasing up proposals sent out yesterday, chasing up leads.
6. 3.00 to 5.30 – sending out that day's proposals, making presentations, attending visits, more canvassing, other meetings and so on.
7. 5.30 – daily figure-taking by the manager, and review of each person's performance that day – staff not to leave until this is completed.

The above structure was used by an office-based sales force which made only a few, local client visits. A different, more flexible structure would be needed if your team spends more time on the road. For salespeople who spend almost all their day travelling, set structures are probably not helpful, although you might want to specify the times of the first and last visits of the day, insofar as these fit in with customers' wishes.

As with any structure, you must always allow some flexibility for individual initiative and customer service (that's what selling is all about), but at the same time, retain enough rigidity to maintain order. It is necessary, for instance, for everyone to know that from 9.15 to 11.30 they should be canvassing on the phone, otherwise salespeople will find they prefer to shuffle paperwork, or make less stressful, non-canvassing calls. If the sales manager finds anyone not canvassing, the salesperson can have no excuse! Between 11.30 and 1.00 the structure asks for proposals to be written – this is because they need to be typed and corrected before they are sent out and, in this example, the manager has arranged for admin. to process all proposals provided they are written by 1.00.

The structure for the afternoon is looser, allowing staff to organize their work according to how the day has developed. They are given a set slot for chasing up proposals they sent out yesterday. The daily figure-taking and performance review (say 5 minutes per salesperson) helps focus their efforts, and enables the manager to offer meaningful praise and advice on the spot. It also prevents people dashing out of the door at 5.30!

A NOTE ON INTRODUCING WORKING STRUCTURES

If you do not already have a daily structure, be careful how you introduce one: staff will probably see it as a restriction on their freedom and may strive to make it unworkable. Introduce a structure gradually, and present it as a means of helping, not controlling, them. For instance, if you insist that proposals are only written between 11.30 and 1.00, explain that this will help admin. streamline their work and guarantee same-day production. If you want everyone to canvass from 9.15 to 11.30, explain the benefits: if everyone is canvassing together, then everyone will do their fair share; it will help them 'hit the ground running' in the mornings; it will generate more sales and commission; and it will stop you telling them what they should be doing every day! And always allow some leeway – never let rules prevent your staff helping your customers. And never let rules stand in the way of profit!

MONITORING PERFORMANCE

As a general rule, sales managers should record their staff's performance each day. Without figures you cannot assess or reward your staff's performance, or even tell whether your team is on target. By figures, I mean not just sales revenue figures (they only tell you the end-result), but figures which reflect the volume and quality of work done each day, such as:

- number of telephone calls made
- number of proposals sent out (or equivalent)
- number of visits arranged
- number and value of sales made
- number of outstanding bids, offers (or equivalent).

Without this sort of data, you will be unable to analyse what an individual salesperson's problems or strengths may be. Just by taking the figures, you will find that performance improves because, if nothing else, it helps staff become aware of how much, or how little, they are achieving. It also shows them how much more the top performers are able to achieve. If you can publish 'best figures' each day, so much the better – often top performers are the highest achievers simply because they work the hardest, and it does no harm for everyone else to know this.

For a full consideration of evaluating and monitoring your staff's performance, see Chapters 8 and 9.

SUMMARY

This chapter shows that your staff will perform better if they are given clear instructions and goals, and if they are monitored systematically and constructively. In the following chapter we will examine ways of assessing and directing staff by means of goal-setting and reviews.

5

GOAL-SETTING, REVIEWS, PROMOTION AND DISCIPLINE

In this chapter we look at ways of improving motivation and boosting productivity through the use of individual goal-setting, reviews and effective discipline and promotion. The subjects we cover are as follows:

- Constructive goal-setting
- Make goal-setting work!
- Reviews
- Handling complaints and grievances
- Discipline
- Promotions
- Team structure.

CONSTRUCTIVE GOAL-SETTING

Goal-setting enables you to:

- Find out how your staff are feeling.
- Predict how well each person will perform.
- Agree with each person their monthly performance targets.
- Discuss any personal or professional issues in private.

Conducting monthly goal-settings with your staff does not simply mean telling each person how many sales they must achieve. Goal-setting is worthless without (i) getting your staff's *agreement* to achieve their goals, and (ii) showing your staff *how* they can achieve them. Goal-setting therefore involves two elements:

- Reviewing all aspects of the salesperson's performance – the number of calls made, the quality of their paperwork, the number of meetings and visits – and setting goals or guidelines for whichever of these will help the person achieve his or her overall target.
- Agreeing targets with the contribution and commitment of the salesperson.

It follows that to be able to run constructive, credible goal-settings, you must first have an established means of collecting accurate data about your staff's activities. (For more details of this topic, see 'Monitoring performance' in Chapter 4, and most of Chapters 8 and 9.)

The following is a good goal-setting format:

1. On the first day of each sales period (let's assume it's a month), hold a goal-setting meeting with each salesperson in private.
2. Review with them their performance over the previous three months, concentrating on last month's results, and *ask them* to explain why they have done as well (or as badly) as they have. Listen to what they have to say. Encourage them to review themselves – every good salesperson will do this anyway, and it is a good habit to acquire. What can we learn from their recent performance? Is there any improvement, or falling off? What do they think their strengths and weaknesses are? Always ask – don't just tell them. What should their aims be in the coming month?
3. Don't just review the person's sales figures – look at the figures behind the sales figures: the number of phone-calls made, the number of letters sent, appointments made, bids won and lost. If you ask salespeople to account for their whole performance (whether it is good or bad) you will receive vague, unhelpful answers, but if you ask them to explain the low number of phone-calls they made, or the high number of appointments, you will get a real answer, which will help them – and you – understand how they are working. It may be a good idea to compare the salesperson's figures to the team's average, or even to one of the high performers, to show them where they're doing well, and where they could improve.
4. Goal-settings are the ideal occasion for offering praise, constructive criticism, and discussing a person's career aspirations – use them to build bonds between you and your staff. Always balance criticism with praise and, wherever possible, always offer criticism which is constructive: that is, tell the person how they can improve, not simply what they are doing wrong.
5. Keep the meeting warm, friendly and encouraging, except where a person's performance has been unsatisfactory and you need to make this clear. Here you must be frank and honest.
6. Now we come to the goal-setting itself. You already need to have a precise idea of how much business you require from each salesperson that month. You will also know whether they are likely to exceed this or not. Ask the salesperson how well he/she thinks they can do this month. Start with the figures: how many phone-calls can they make (the same, more, less?), how many appointments? If you can get their commitment to make 10 per cent more phone-calls and consequently arrange 10 per cent as many appointments, you should be able to expect 10 per cent more sales. Conclude by asking them what sales they think they will achieve. In most cases you will have the figure you want.
7. Whatever goals you decide to set, express them in as clear and tangible a form as possible, otherwise they will mean nothing to the person involved: telling them to 'improve their performance' or make more company visits is too vague, and impossible for you or them to assess fairly.
8. Ask the person if they agree with the goal. It is important you get their commitment and that they feel it is realistic and achievable.
9. Record details of the goal and your conversation for future reference. Give your salesperson a written copy.

Once you have established goal-setting as part of your monthly routine, you will find it helps you in many different ways – to motivate the workforce, to keep in touch with how people are feeling, to talk to people in private without it appearing unusual, and many more.

MAKE GOAL-SETTING WORK!

If you set targets on a monthly basis, assess your staff's performance after two weeks – are they all on course, or are some falling behind? Now is the time to talk to them about it – not at the end of the month! Perhaps you and they will have to reappraise their goals, or perhaps if they work harder (or better), they will make up the difference. Whatever you do, do not just ignore matters if a goal is either not being met or has become, for whatever reason, unrealistic. It is better to downscale an unrealistic goal and insist that the salesperson achieves this, than to have him or her give up completely when something is unachievable. (See the section on 'Expectancy Theory' in the Appendix to Chapter 3.)

Make it clear that you will use goal-settings to help determine your staff's success or failure in their jobs as a whole. Once your staff realize that goal-setting is not a meaningless ritual but something which you take seriously and which affects their careers, you will find fewer people fall behind, and their accuracy in predicting future sales will increase.

At the next goal-setting, use the previous month's goal-setting as your starting-point: was it achieved, and if not, why not? This is all part of the process of making staff take more responsibility for their performance. If the goal was not achieved, you must give concrete, practical advice as to how the salesperson can avoid this next time: telling them to just 'work harder' is useless unless, for instance, you can show that they do less work than they could, or work fewer hours than their colleagues.

REVIEWS

Reviews should follow on naturally from goal-settings. Unfortunately, reviews can sometimes be stiff, formal occasions, with both parties saying what is expected of them, not what they actually think. Regular goal-settings help avoid this by giving you detailed evidence of the person's performance and by getting both of you used to talking together.

You should review staff regularly but not so regularly that reviews become meaningless. Once every six months is usually right. It is best to review all the staff at the same time. This prevents any one member of staff feeling 'overlooked' and enables you to announce promotions simultaneously, which can avoid unnecessary jealousy. Fixed review times also stop an over-ambitious salesperson pushing management into an early review – these things do happen!

Conducting staff appraisals and reviews is an art in itself and there are many books written on the subject. The following are the main points:

O Give your staff advance warning of reviews and suggest they prepare for them by reviewing their own performance and any issues they would like raised. Never spring an important review on an employee.

O Make your own written preparation beforehand. Topics should include:

- Their performance: sales, quality and quantity of work, goals and so on. Are you happy with it?
- Their team contribution
- Their motivation and ambitions
- Their happiness
- Their good points: what can they build on?
- Their bad points: what must they improve?
- What happens next? Is a promotion or payrise in order, or should this be conditional on future performance and so on?
- How do you think the person will respond to the review? Can you foresee problems?
- Is there anything else to discuss?

- Allow plenty of time for the review and do not let anyone interrupt it – the reviewee must feel they are the centre of your attention.
- Start the review by putting the person at ease and briefly praising or congratulating them (if this is due). Then ask them to review their own performance. Listen to how they perceive their efforts. Do not interrupt, but you could nod, make brief comments of agreement or encouragement. Make notes.
- Make sure you understand their points. Is there anything you are not sure about? How do they feel? Do they enjoy their work? Where do they see themselves going from here? What areas of self-improvement have they set themselves? What goals do they have?
- Once you know the state of the salesperson's feelings and self-perception, you can decide how the rest of the review will progress. Do you agree with them? Or do you think they are wrong?
- If you agree, things should progress smoothly. Offer praise, encouragement and advice where appropriate.
- If you disagree, or if the salesperson's performance has been unsatisfactory, things may be less straightforward. How you handle this will depend on your judgement. This subject is covered fully in the section on discipline later in this chapter. However, here is a framework for constructively disciplining a person as part of their review:
    - Always present the facts as clearly and objectively as possible. Compare performance to the team's average or to the minimum performance standards you have set.
    - State clearly and frankly that you are displeased/disappointed with the person's performance and the reasons why.
    - Make sure the person understands.
    - Give the person goals or a set of tasks which will rectify this situation.
    - Insist that these goals are met, and state the consequences of failure to meet them (for example, ineligibility for review, formal warning, dismissal).
    - Get their agreement to achieve these goals.
- Often, in a normal review, such proceedings will not be necessary: you may simply need to bring certain matters to the person's attention (whether it is lack of punctuality, or poor documentation, or lack of sales confidence):
    - Explain that it is one of the few things holding back their progress, or restricting their earnings (couch this in terms relevant to that person's position and personality).
    - Ask if they are able – and willing – to improve in this area.
    - Ask how long they think you should give them to make this improvement. Salespeople invariably give short periods of time or say 'I can do this straight away', and this is the easiest way of generating their commitment to act on your advice. If you think the time-scale is impractical or too short, say so, and help them suggest a more sensible solution.
    - Then tell them you are pleased with their answer. Let them feel good about agreeing to solve their problem.
- If a salesperson has a weakness which they cannot solve themselves (for example poor canvassing skills), it is up to you to make suggestions. Usually offering additional coaching time (outside office hours) shows you are willing to help – and draws out more from your staff. Or seat him/her next to a salesperson who is strong in this area. Or offer to go through that problem with them each time it arises, as soon as it arises. See *Training the Sales Team*, the companion volume to this book, for more suggestions and further material on this topic.

GOAL-SETTING, REVIEWS, PROMOTION AND DISCIPLINE   45

- If you want to make constructive criticisms, but within the context of a positive, generally upbeat review, sandwich your criticism between two statements of praise, like this: praise – criticism – praise. To end a review on a critical note can leave the salesperson feeling negative and demotivated.
- Before the end of the review give the person the chance to talk about their future: where would they like to go with the company? What are their ambitions? Are they happy at the moment? Is there anything you could do which would improve their situation? This is vital to building loyalty and long-term commitment.
- Leave the salesperson feeling positive, optimistic and valued as an individual.

HANDLING COMPLAINTS AND GRIEVANCES

Sometimes in your reviews, or in the course of your daily work, you will be faced with complaints and grievances. Knowing how to handle these is part of maintaining the smooth running and motivation of your team. Always make yourself approachable on any matters about which staff may have complaints. If you implement difficult changes, or make tough decisions, let staff know that if they have 'any particular concerns' (a useful euphemism), they are welcome to see you in private. If you actively discourage complaints, you may well cause resentment to build up to exploding point.

HOW TO HANDLE COMPLAINTS AND GRIEVANCES

The following is a step-by-step guide:

- When approached with a complaint or grievance, listen carefully to the person and show yourself genuinely concerned. If necessary, write down the details.
- As well as listening to the details of the complaint, try to form an understanding of the motive behind the complaint. Is it simply a genuine grievance, or has it arisen for other more personal reasons, such as a fear of failure? Staff will sometimes complain to generate more attention or reassurance from management, or to discuss their chances of promotion and so on. Do you need to address these needs as well?
- Decide whether to handle this situation now or to arrange a time when it may be more convenient, or more private, or after you have had a chance to consider your approach. If you do arrange a time, ask for the person's agreement and keep to the time punctually. Never postpone complaints which are urgent or strongly felt.
- Usually complaints arise because a rule or established procedure appears to have been broken. Refer to this rule or principle, and assess its actual *purpose*: what is its point?
- Assess the current situation: does this rule apply here, and if so, how? Has the rule been broken? Do you think the person's complaint is justified?
- Discuss this with the person. It may be simply a question of explaining that the rule does not apply in this case, or is not relevant. Or it may involve agreeing that the rule has been violated, and that there is something you need to put right.
- Agree the action. If the complaint is justified, agree with the person how you will rectify it. If you are personally to blame, apologize, and ask if your apology is accepted. If the complaint has proved to be groundless, make sure the person is happy to let the matter rest there.
- Rectify the grievance. Do this as soon as possible.
- Record the conversation and any steps taken for future reference.
- Plan for the future. How can you stop this happening again?

Sometimes staff will make complaints about other members of the team. These cannot be ignored, but must be handled with particular tact. Listen seriously and sensitively to the complaint, but pay particular attention to the possible cause: could the person be motivated by envy (of the person's success or their popularity), or insecurity, or have they been insulted in some way? Or is it a fair and reasonable complaint?

Show yourself sympathetic but, as a general rule, don't commit yourself to a particular course of action until you have spoken to the other person. Usually, you should not disclose the source of the complaint to this person, and you must do everything you can to minimize the spitefulness, resentment and demotivation which complaints can cause. Once you have talked to the person concerned, you should form your own judgement. Then see the complainant and explain to him/her the steps you have taken, and ask if they are content with that.

DISCIPLINE

Inevitably some reviews involve discipline, or a need for discipline may arise following poor performance or behaviour. It helps if you have an established method of disciplining staff. This gives you a framework within which you can express yourself confidently and define what happens next on your own terms. It also protects you from overreacting to situations or any accusations of victimization. In this section we examine:

O General principles of discipline
O How to discipline.

GENERAL PRINCIPLES OF DISCIPLINE

O Staff should always have a clear idea of what standards of performance and behaviour are expected of them. Therefore, discipline, if necessary, does not come as a shock.
O If you can see a salesperson behaving or performing in a way that may lead to discipline, warn them (in private) and ask them to explain themselves. If it is a question of performance, the sooner you tell someone, and the more concerned you show yourself to help, the better.
O Do not discipline people unnecessarily. Never appear to enjoy disciplining people, but don't apologize: after all, it's their fault, not yours.
O Conduct all discipline procedures in private and allow yourself plenty of time to discuss the matter.
O Before disciplining someone, plan the meeting as you would for a review:

 – What is the problem?
 – Why do you think this problem exists?
 – How can this be solved?
 – Is any disciplinary action appropriate?
 – What happens next?

O Define punishments to fit the situation. Acts of gross insubordination may warrant instant dismissal, but you must decide whether this serves *your interests*: do you want to set a clear example? Or do you wish to play the incident down?
O How do you value your staff? All discipline and punishment must be fair, but it also has to be pragmatic. It is a fact of life that, for minor offences at least, you will probably want to discipline your top performers less harshly than your poor performers, – which may lead to accusations of favouritism. In these circumstances, defuse the

GOAL-SETTING, REVIEWS, PROMOTION AND DISCIPLINE 47

situation by stating that in all disciplinary matters you take a person's overall performance into consideration – isn't this the same as the law? Only in extreme cases should such considerations be irrelevant.

- Never be afraid to discipline. Lack of discipline leads to loss of morale.
- What sort of punishments are suitable for what sort of problems? They will depend on the nature of your company and the relevant legal guidelines. Never take any disciplinary action which may result in dismissal without consulting your personnel department on correct procedure. Generally speaking, all staff need to be given warnings – usually two written ones – before it is safe to dismiss them. This procedure protects you legally, gives the salesperson every chance to improve, and shows the rest of the team that you are acting fairly. Within sales the most non-contestable ground for dismissal is failure to achieve sales targets. This should be clearly stated in your staff's job description (see Chapter 4 for full details).
- When you have to dismiss staff, it is usually best to announce this decision yourself to the sales team (obviously after you have told the person concerned). If you are nervous or appear furtive, it will seem that *you* have done something wrong. Say why you have had to dismiss the person. Make it clear that you regret doing so, but that you were left with no alternative. Sometimes dismissals can unsettle a sales team, and you may want to remind them how well they are doing, and make it clear that this dismissal is, you hope, an isolated example. After this sort of announcement, always make yourself available for consultation. You might want to see certain people (the person's close friends or team-mates) in private to reconfirm their loyalty.

HOW TO DISCIPLINE

Here are guidelines for conducting disciplinary reviews:

1. Start by stating the problem as you see it. Make your opinion as objective as possible by comparing the person's performance to the minimum standards you have set, or the levels agreed in goal-setting.
2. Ask the person what they think the problem is and why it has arisen. How can they solve it?
3. Listen to them. Perhaps they are right. Or perhaps they are making excuses. If they are, you must confront this clearly and frankly. This is usually best done by:
   (i) showing that other team-members do not have these problems,
   (ii) pointing out any inconsistency in the excuse,
   (iii) simply stating what you think the real problem is, and
   (iv) saying you are not interested in whether there is a valid excuse; your sole concern is that this problem is solved. You can put this bluntly as follows: if the person is saying that no one could do any better in their position, then presumably they are saying their position is no longer viable and should be closed.
4. If your salesperson has glaring faults which must be corrected, or if he/she seems unaware of the seriousness of the problem, you must ask them how committed they are to the job, and how hard they are prepared to work to turn these results around. You must spell out what will happen if they fail to improve. This is vital. There is no point in disciplining a poor performer and trying to persuade them to improve if you do not have their sincere commitment – and do not make it clear to them how important this is.
5. Once you have that commitment, agree with them a specific course of action, with specific goals which *must* be achieved within precise time-scales (for example,

number of calls a day, number of appointments made). Sometimes the person can devise these goals for themselves; usually, however, you will set them yourself (this shows that this discussion is quite different from normal goal-setting). Give the goals strict time-scales, and define them in terms which can be objectively assessed. Avoid subjective guidelines such as 'better phonework'; prefer such measurable criteria as 'at least 60 per cent effective phone-calls' or 'at least 40 canvass calls a day by 11.00 am'.

6 Whatever goals you set, make sure the person understands them (state them in writing).
7 Agree the goals with the person.
8 Tell the person to refer back to you at certain stages of the sales process so that you can monitor, support and advise them on their performance.
9 Make it quite clear what will happen if they do not meet these goals. And also what will happen if they do: will this be the end of the disciplinary process or will they need to be set further goals until you are sure the problem is solved?
10 In certain circumstances, you should ask the person whether they feel they have been fairly treated, and whether they think they will be able to make these improvements. This reduces ill will, and reaffirms their commitment.

Give your staff encouragement and help to meet their disciplinary goals. Be pleased for them when they do, and congratulate them. Always meet with them to review their performance at the time set and assess their performance according to the criteria you have already laid down. If they have improved, ask them why, and see if you can reinforce any good working practices or attitudes. If they still have problems, suggest further solutions. Agree what happens next, and if possible, conclude the meeting on a positive note. Above all else, recognize and reward positive attitude and commitment: this is the most important ingredient in overcoming problems positively.

PROMOTIONS

If you want to ensure the long-term motivation and commitment of your staff you have to offer them a career path. The benefits of promoting your staff should be self-evident, but we will briefly review them:

- Loyalty: You will build staff loyalty through promoting them regularly and fairly.
- Skill development: Promotion enables staff to develop their skills, in turn making them more valuable members of staff.
- Job satisfaction and interest: Promotion should make work more rewarding and stimulating.
- Praise: Promotion is a public recognition of success.
- Prestige: Promotion satisfies people's need to feel important.
- Gratitude: Staff will be personally obligated to you.
- Career development: Staff want to work for companies which enable them to develop their careers.
- Team spirit: Promotions create a winning team.
- Reward: Promotion rewards high performers with better packages and salaries than might otherwise be possible.
- Improved administration: Senior staff can perform additional administrative or organizational tasks. They can save you time.
- Better performance: Senior staff can contribute to the morale and working practices of the rest of the staff.

All staff should know how they can gain promotion (ideally this should be in their job description), and they should know the benefits and responsibilities attached. All members of staff should be given every encouragement to achieve promotion. Salespeople should be told their likelihood of future promotion, and how they can achieve this.

Promotions (and assessments for promotions) should be conducted as part of the review process, either on an annual or six-monthly basis. They should be announced publicly and are a good opportunity for general office celebrations and morale-boosting meetings: everyone should feel good, not just the person being promoted.

In the next section we explore how to make promotions work for you and your staff, and different ways of using senior staff within the framework of the team.

TEAM STRUCTURE

You should regularly review the career structure your company provides. Your two aims must be to offer your staff more satisfying careers, and to organize your workforce in the most efficient and effective way possible. The following are good questions to ask:

- What tasks could senior staff do which either I do (and wish I didn't), or which are not done at all?
- What tasks could they perform more effectively than is currently possible?
- How could a better team structure raise morale, streamline administration, improve customer service or boost sales?
- Do we offer a three- to five-year career path to someone joining us?
- Is our career path satisfying? If not, why not? Why do we lose salespeople to other organizations? (See Chapter 11 for more thoughts on this.)
- How could their careers be enhanced?
- What sort of responsibilities can I delegate to people and would this make the position more or less attractive?
- Can I allow senior staff more freedom of action, or is all decision-making in the hands of senior management?

The last three questions highlight the meaning of promotion. For promotion to a senior position to be meaningful it must contain at least one of the following:

- more decision-making
- accountability, either for self or others
- greater freedom to define and pursue own goals
- management or supervision of others
- different position in the reporting structure
- different type or quality of work
- different type of product or service to sell
- better working conditions
- more expectations (and rewards to match)
- more respect from senior management and junior staff.

Whether you are reviewing your current team structure or are seeking to create new levels, bear these issues in mind.

Here are some ways in which new positions can be used productively:

- Would it help your clients if a senior sales executive – or even an account manager or regional sales director – were appointed to look after their account? This is a way titles can win you business, and enhance your staff's feelings of importance.

- Who is responsible for inducting new team-members? Could salespeople be more involved in this? Can senior salespeople 'tutor' or 'counsel' trainees, offering general advice and support, and reporting back to you on their progress? For more information on this, see *Training the Sales Team*, the companion volume to this book.
- Are there new business development roles which would give your staff more opportunity for initiative – and might make cold calling seem more glamorous? If there are, make sure to give the new business consultant some sort of extra scope: different business cards, more freedom to negotiate, travel expenses, clothes allowances, perhaps even a small advertising budget, and so on.
- By creating group leader roles you can harness salespeople's energies (even neutralize boisterous behaviour) by making them accountable for a small group of one to three other salespeople. Pay overriding commission on the group hitting certain targets. Get group leaders to run weekly group meetings to assess performance. Make them responsible for organizing such things as new lead chasing, client servicing rotas, after-sales follow-ups and so on. Being that much closer to the staff than the sales manager (and seeing things when the manager's back is turned), group leaders can ensure these tasks are pursued with more vigour and thoroughness.
- Group leaders or senior sales executives should have regular monthly meetings with the sales manager. These meetings should be frank and open – a discussion between equals. Important topics should be: company morale; a group-by-group report on performance, sales conditions, motivation and so on; do any salespeople have motivational or sales problems? are senior staff aware of any problems? Tell group leaders what you expect of them and how they are performing. Inform them of developments in company policy which they should know. Also use them as a sounding-board for new ideas before launching them on the sales force as a whole.
- Can you involve senior staff in interviewing new recruits? This can build a greater sense of team spirit, and can get staff to have more confidence in the calibre of recruits. (See Chapter 12 for more details.)
- Can senior staff be responsible for monitoring staff's lunchbreaks, ensuring that the phones are answered, keeping tabs on late arrivals?

Depending on your organization, other types of promotion may be possible, perhaps due to expansion or through vacancies arising in other divisions, departments or offices. Never be reluctant to recommend someone for promotion outside of your team or department: if you do not, you will cause resentment by restricting your staff's careers. If you do, people will want to work well for you as they know you will help them. Never begrudge your salespeople their success.

SENIOR JOB DESCRIPTIONS

Whatever the structure of your sales force, be sure to define senior positions, with their responsibilities and benefits, on paper, in separate job descriptions. Don't just list senior staff's responsibilities: define the limits of their authority and accountability as well. Be sure to respect the distinctions between staff. There is nothing worse than a manager who ignores the positions his/her staff hold – except when it suits him or her. And remember, if promotion entails increased responsibilities and longer hours, make sure your staff are properly compensated.

AVOID EMPTY TITLES

Sometimes promoting staff can lead to cynicism and demotivation if the titles do not make any difference to their role and status within the company. One sales company was the exception to this: they were not able to offer their staff genuine career prospects but found they could retain them for longer by creating titles for them. And up to a point, the staff were happy with this 'arrangement', as they received benefits from promotion and enhanced their c.v.'s for when they did finally move.

This exception notwithstanding, promotion should be treated with the greatest attention. Especially in sales, a company's future will depend on the calibre of staff it is able to train, retain and develop.

SUMMARY

In this chapter, we have examined the ways of improving your staff's motivation and performance by the use of goal-settings and reviews, and how they can be rewarded or punished with promotion or discipline. It could be argued that these subjects form the core of the sales manager's job, as it is in exercising these functions that you have greatest control over, and communication with, your staff, and are most able to influence their attitude and output. In the next chapter we study the subject of communication in more detail.

6

COMMUNICATION

In Chapter 1, we saw that one of the key skills of leadership is the ability to communicate with your staff. This chapter offers practical advice on how to communicate effectively and motivationally. In particular, it focuses on how to manage productive and successful sales meetings. It is divided into two sections:

○ How to communicate
○ Managing the sales meeting.

HOW TO COMMUNICATE

Communication is at the heart of the sales manager's job. If you cannot communicate your goals effectively and attractively, your staff will lack direction. If you cannot communicate your advice and judgements, your staff will not know how to achieve your goals. If you cannot communicate with your staff, your staff will not communicate with you.

Sales managers should communicate with their staff regularly, and provide them with a stream of motivational news, advice and encouragement. Changes should, generally speaking, be signposted clearly (see Chapter 2 for details on 'Managing change'). Your sales team should be given constant feedback about how well they are doing (keep this positive). Without this reassurance, staff will quickly lose their sense of purpose, progress, and self-confidence.

Managers should take care not to give staff too much information (this can be confusing and time-consuming), nor information which is ambiguous or unclear. The following check-list might be helpful:

❖ **What do I want to communicate?** Before saying or doing anything you must have a clear idea of your long-term *goals*, how you want to achieve them (your *means*), and your immediate concern (your *message*).

❖ **How relevant is my message?** Don't waste your staff's time – and lose their attention. Make sure you present your message so that it is *helpful*, *useful*, and *relevant*.

❖ **What is my situation?** Is your message urgent? Are the staff going to be motivated or demoralized? What problems can you foresee? Try to anticipate objections and prepare your answers. If your message may touch a raw nerve, think of how you can reduce the risk of being 'taken the wrong way'.

- ❖ **How can I communicate?** Assess the options at your disposal. These are considered later in this chapter.

- ❖ **What preparations should I make?** If you are about to announce sweeping changes to your team, you may need to consult with your senior staff first. You may want to prepare visual aids or information hand-outs.

- ❖ **How can I reinforce my message?** If you have an important message, you can reinforce it: by reminding staff in your conversations with them, distributing hand-outs, using memos, by altering your own working practices, including it in future reviews, and so on.

- ❖ **Am I understood?** Don't just assume that if you tell someone something, they will understand you. Communication breakdowns often occur because: the speaker was not clear; the audience did not pay attention; the speaker was communicating an emotional or controversial issue and the audience heard either what it wanted to hear or what it was afraid of hearing; the speaker did not relate the importance of the message to the rest of work; the speaker did not ask for feedback.

- ❖ **Give me feedback.** Communication must be a two-way process. Encourage and ask for response to your message. This will show if your message was understood, and provides you with essential information.

DIFFERENT MEANS OF COMMUNICATING

A good sales manager will use many different forms of communication. The most important are:

- Sales Meetings
- Memos
- Goal-settings and reviews
- Informal discussion
- Appearance and conduct.

Sales meetings occupy the second half of this chapter. Memos can convey short messages and updates. Memos should be short, punchy and deal with one point only. Send regular memos as a way of keeping in touch, but if you send too many, none will be read. Memos are best for reinforcing points made at sales meetings or for reminding staff of working practices. Do not send memos announcing major changes or controversial developments. Memos should be clearly headed so that staff can instantly see their significance and relevance.

Goal-settings and reviews are excellent opportunities for communicating with your staff on a one-to-one basis. They are particularly effective for communicating personal praise and criticism, sounding staff out on sensitive issues, or for persuading them of the virtue of a course of action. They also enable you to tap into the grapevine.

Informal discussion occurs almost whenever you talk to your sales force: be aware of it and use it. Always understand what general message you are trying to convey and avoid saying or doing anything that undermines this. In your conversations with your staff you should be constantly reinforcing and restating your views.

Appearance and conduct often communicate more than words. For this reason you should take great care about how you dress and groom yourself. Remember that you will not be able to convince staff that all is well, or you have their best interests at heart, if you march around the office scowling and frowning. Project confidence and success. Smile. Be aware of your body language: keep your actions open, expansive, dynamic; do not retreat into a shell or appear nervous or defensive.

MANAGING THE SALES MEETING

Sales meetings are the best way to communicate with the team as a whole and get their feedback. They are also the single most effective means available to you of controlling, informing, motivating and leading the sales team. Here are some of the functions of the sales meeting:

- To build team spirit
- To present team goals and targets
- To announce or implement change
- To announce promotions
- As a discussion group to generate new ideas or debate courses of action
- To give group encouragement and rally the sales team
- To provide training and opportunities for problem-solving
- To generate feedback from the sales floor
- To give individuals the chance to address the rest of the team
- To allow staff to present reports on their group's progress.

One of the sales manager's main priorities should be to organize and run regular and effective sales meetings.

Whether you have sales meetings every day or every week, once a fortnight or once a month, will depend on your market and the amount of information you and the team have to convey and share. As a general rule, meetings are best held on a weekly basis, although in some highly pressurized sales environments, daily meetings to help everyone get started at the beginning of the day are a better idea.

SETTING THE AGENDA

- Go through the check-list for communicating with your staff at the beginning of this chapter (see pages 53–4): what are your *goals, means* and *message*? What is your *situation*? What *problems* do you foresee?

- Always write out the agenda in advance, and make notes of your key points. Allow space for staff to ask questions or for you to expand on points. Make sure the meeting has a positive beginning and a positive finale.

- The following are all subjects which could form part of your sales meeting:
    - Report by you on the team's performance (praise, encouragement and so on)
    - Problems you think need addressing
    - Opportunities you think can be exploited
    - Any corporate or team news
    - Changes you want to implement
    - Changes you would like the team to debate
    - Problems you would like to discuss
    - Training material
    - Market or product information
    - Reports presented by other members of staff
    - Announcements of promotions, competitions, awards and so on.

PLANNING THE SALES MEETING

- Announce a definite time, location and length for each meeting – ensure that all staff can and will attend.

56 LEADING THE SALES TEAM

- Meetings must be run punctually and should be short and to the point: 30 minutes for a weekly sales meeting is usually sufficient. Meetings should be held at the same time and location each week. They should not clash with prime selling time.

- How can you support your meeting with visual aids? Can you employ written reports, flipcharts, diagrams, photographs and so on? Prepare and distribute handouts where suitable.

- Can you involve other members of your team in the meeting? Are there reports or information you can ask them to prepare beforehand?

RUNNING THE SALES MEETING

- The key factors in sales meetings are *pace, delivery* and *mood*. Keep meetings upbeat, present them enthusiastically and audibly, respond to your audience's mood.

- Make it clear that you have an agenda. As a general rule, you should give copies of this to your staff before the meeting, unless there are 'controversial' topics which you would rather introduce personally and without warning. Sometimes forewarning your staff will simply make them unduly nervous or argumentative.

- Expect all your staff to be punctual. The only excuse for being late is making a sale – ensure that that is quite clear.

- Do not allow staff to receive phone calls during the meeting. Arrange for someone else to take messages.

- Encourage questions and discussion where appropriate, but don't appear apprehensive or uncertain. Don't let meetings consist of a ten-minute speech from you telling the staff what they should be doing. People will find it boring – and patronizing.

- Involve members of the team. Ask individuals for reports, or ask people to comment on the current sales situation (for example, 'What do you think the main problem is, Mark?'). Ask specific questions, and ask specific people. If you do this skilfully, it can be a good way of praising staff and helping them gain greater job satisfaction (for example, 'Why do you think you're able to make so many appointments at the moment, Clare?' or 'How do you get around this objection, Bill?').

- Chair discussions. Do not let one person's opinion predominate. Make sure that a balanced view is expressed. Summarize key points.

- If you are discussing plans for the future, or are resolving problems, conclude by stating what happens next and what actions you will take.

- Never put matters to the vote – this sets a precedent which limits your power to make decisions. Simply thank staff for their views and say you will take them into consideration when deciding on a solution.

- Enjoy sales meetings. If you don't, no one else will.

IMPLEMENTING CHANGE

- If you have to announce or implement important changes at a sales meeting, it is important not to demoralize the staff or let the meeting become confrontational.

- If you can foresee problems coming from certain people, it may be good to talk to them in advance and find a way of reassuring or neutralizing them (or if all else

- fails, simply telling them to keep their views to themselves). For more information, see the notes on 'The Guardian of the Norms' in Chapter 3.

- Start by describing the current situation to staff, reminding them of any problems and why they cannot be allowed to continue.

- You might then throw the question open to them, even if you have already decided on a solution: how would they solve these problems? This enables them to see the situation from your perspective.

- You might feel that discussion could create more problems. In which case tell your staff you have reviewed all options, and want to 'introduce a solution' or 'make some improvements' (both these phrases are non-threatening). Announce the change clearly and simply (save details for later) and then immediately summarize the benefits.

- Ask for any questions or if they have any concerns. Unless you can easily and unambiguously answer these, say: 'I'm glad you mentioned that; don't worry, that is being taken care of'. This shows you are concerned for your staff's well-being without committing you to any course of action.

- Give your staff clear time-scales for change.

- Make change non-threatening, by offering training, support, emphasizing benefits, or by telling staff they will not be assessed in this new area for the first few weeks.

- Confirm the change in writing. The details of how change will be implemented often confuse matters and, where time-scale permits, are usually best explained at the following meeting or on a one-to-one basis.

PROBLEMS ASSOCIATED WITH SALES MEETINGS

- When staff are demoralized or angry, meetings can become confrontational or negative. Be prepared for this, but don't dodge the issues: if the staff have a grievance, or are feeling despondent, it's your job to either tackle the root of the problem, or to convince them their attitude *is* the problem!

- If your staff need reassurance, show them you understand their concern. Tell them what steps you have already taken, ask them to suggest solutions and promise to look into them.

- But if your team are feeling demoralized through their own fault, be honest and tell them so – that's what sales meetings are for! Sometimes salespeople need to be told that they cannot blame their poor performance on the market or the product, but on themselves, or their lack of work or self-belief. If you have to be critical, keep your criticism general, not personal (save personal criticisms for one to one talks directly after the meeting), and offer constructive solutions to the problems.

- Sometimes staff will ask you to justify some unpopular piece of policy (for example, 'Why do we have to . . ?'). Often the best response is to ask back: 'Why do you think?' or 'What was the reason I just gave?' The person has to answer or risk looking foolish.

- If someone is being deliberately obtuse or belligerent to provoke you into an argument, don't be drawn in. Ask to see the person in your office either after the meeting, or after work, when they've had a chance to think things over. Remember, other members of staff don't like a colleague who is deliberately obstructive and you will enhance your standing by staying calm and reasonable.

- ❖ Do not mistake someone with genuine concerns for a troublemaker. Don't become over-defensive every time someone disagrees with you in public: give them a fair answer. And don't panic (or waffle) if you cannot answer a difficult question: simply say 'That's a good question – I'll come back to you on that'.

- ❖ You will have fewer problems at meetings if you carefully prepare your agenda beforehand and keep the meeting to a strict time-scale.

- ❖ When you lead the meeting, anticipate the most obvious concerns and objections in your talk, and try to pre-empt problems.

SUMMARY

Communication takes place in every meeting, every conversation with your staff. Make sure it is effective, positive and conveys your message. Aim for clarity in everything. Staff should have a clear understanding of your goals, your message and your opinions. Regular constructive sales meetings will give both you and your staff greater opportunities for communication and a greater sense of common purpose.

7
COMMISSION SCHEMES AND PRIZES

In this chapter we review the two ways in which you can reward and motivate your staff materially: commission schemes and prizes.

INTRODUCTION

In sales there is no such thing as average effort. The difference between poor and excellent performance can often be the difference between no sales and a full order book. Your salespeople recognize this, and for them to work hard and perform well, they will have to see their efforts, ability and performance rewarded *according to their results*. As Chapter 3 shows, on occasions, this 'reward' may be praise, or recognition, job satisfaction or pride in one's work, or may arise from belief in a common goal or team spirit. Usually, the reward will be money or some other form of financial or material benefit. Prizes are an excellent means of rewarding and encouraging outstanding achievement. But the only fair way of consistently and regularly repaying all of your staff for their contributions is through your commission scheme.

SALES COMMISSION SCHEMES

A good commission scheme should do the following:

- Reward excellent performance generously (and thereby encourage it)
- Enable average performers to earn an average wage and encourage them to earn more
- Give everyone incentive to do even better
- Be based on individual (NOT group or team) targets and performance
- Define minimum standards of performance.

Exactly how you devise your scheme will depend on your market. In some types of financial consultancy, for instance, earnings are solely commission-based; in other areas employees receive a basic salary which enables them to live, and then look to their commission to provide them with a suitable lifestyle.

Most companies have a fixed rate of commission and fixed targets (the same for all salespeople); some have more flexible and subjective approaches. We review various options below, but first here are some general principles:

- **Commission must motivate and reward high earners:** In almost all sales teams, the majority of sales are generated by the top 25 per cent of the sales force. Commission schemes should reward these people first and foremost.
- **Commission must be based on individual performance:** Commission based on group performance discourages individuals from doing better than average. It underpays your top performers, and overpays your poorest. For the benefit of team unity, you may choose to reward staff with additional overriding team bonuses.
- **Commission schemes should be directly related to revenue:** That is, they must directly relate to the amount or the value of sales a person generates. They should not have ceilings, not be 'stepped' in a way which discourages staff to earn more.
- **Commission schemes should help staff prioritize their work:** Staff will work hardest to achieve the results which will earn them commission. When designing your commission scheme, make sure you are encouraging the right activities and results. Usually commission is paid on the actual cash value of sales generated, but sometimes this may make staff too short-sighted, and it might be better to pay commission on the volume of sales or take into account the importance of repeat or new business.

TYPES OF SCHEMES

Below are examples of commission schemes commonly used, together with brief comments on their advantages and disadvantages.

Simple percentage

Company A pays its salespeople 10 per cent of whatever they sell.

- **Advantages:** very easy to administer.
- **Disadvantages:** does not provide any particular indication of what is good or bad performance; company will pay out some commission even on low sales figures.

Target system

Company B does not pay percentages but lump sum bonuses on the following targets:

Sales	Bonuses
£5 000	£500
£7 500	£1 000
£10 000	£1 500
£12 500	£2 250

- **Advantages:** rewards higher performers in particular; it sets a minimum standard (in this case £5 000) and saves money by only paying out if targets are reached.
- **Disadvantages:** staff will be demoralized if they just miss a target and receive nothing.

Sliding scale

Company C pays commission on a sliding percentage scale as follows:

Sales	Commission
Below £4 000	0%
£4 000 to £8 000	10%
£8 000 to £12 000	15%
£12 000 to £15 000	20%
£15 000 upwards	30%

- **Advantages:** encourages good performance, rewards high performers, sets minimum standards.
- **Disadvantages:** quite complicated to work out.

Rolling target

Company D pays a commission on all monthly sales over £2 500. If this target is not achieved one month, it is added to the next month's target. So if salespeople fail to reach base target in Month 1, they need to get £5 000 in Month 2. And if they fail to reach £5 000 in Month 2, they will need to get £7 500 in Month 3, and so on.

- **Advantages:** demands consistent results from staff, punishes (and does not pay) poor performers.
- **Disadvantages:** if salespeople have a string of bad months, they can be presented with a seemingly impossible task and become more demotivated. This can be avoided by allowing sales from one month to be deducted from the next month's base target. For instance, if a person achieved sales of £1 750 in Month 1, the target for Month 2 would be £3 250 (being £5 000 − £1 750). This can lead to numerous complications and confusions.

Individual targets

Company E agrees with each salesperson their own goals and targets – their commission is based on these.

- **Advantages:** this can take into account easier or harder territories and can be directly related to the salesperson's ability.
- **Disadvantages:** any system which seems to pay one person more than another for the same results will be perceived as unfair.

It is possible to avoid the problem of apparent unfairness. At the beginning of the sales year, the sales manager asks each salesperson to agree their own base quarterly target (within certain realistic guidelines). The higher the target, the higher the salesperson's basic salary, but the harder it is to earn commission. This system has the great merit of getting each salesperson's commitment to their target (and motivation to achieve it).

Here is an example from real life: after they complete their induction, salespeople can choose any base salary for themselves between £10 000 and £20 000 a year. Whatever figure they choose is multiplied by 1.5 to calculate their quarterly target. So if a person chooses a salary of £15 000, he or she has to achieve quarterly sales of £22 500 before he or she can earn commission. The actual commission rate is as follows: as soon as base target is reached, a bonus of £500 is won and 10 per cent commission is then paid on all sales over base target and 20 per cent commission for sales that are 50 per cent over base target. So, taking our quarterly target of £22 500, the salesperson would get 10 per cent of everything over £22 500 within the three-month quarter (as well as the £500 bonus), and 20 per cent of everything over £33 750.

The attraction of this system is that it does not encourage staff to opt for high basic salaries because this makes earning commission even harder. It also removes the need for pay reviews, and gives each member of the team a sense of commitment to the targets. However, the system is very complicated, and needs to be monitored carefully.

Using commission schemes as rewards

Company F offers different goals and commission schemes to its salespeople according to length of service and each person's performance records.

- **Advantages:** an effective and performance-orientated alternative to the usual pay-rise or a promotion, encouraging company loyalty and keeping high performers satisfied.

○   **Disadvantages:** staff may feel that it is not fair; if people find their new commission scheme gives them more money for less performance, they can become demotivated; and the scheme can be complex to administer.

OTHER IDEAS

Many companies use commission schemes to discourage inconsistent results, as inconsistency suggests staff are working only part of the time, or are 'stacking' sales for maximum commission. Even if this is not the case, inconsistent results make sales harder to predict, add more stress to the sales manager's life, and can create cash flow problems. Consequently some companies offer overriding commission on a quarterly or half-yearly basis (this enables them to pay less per month), or they only pay full commission if base target is reached the following month. Both of these are excellent ideas.

PRIZES AND COMPETITIONS

Prizes allow you to:

○   introduce excitement to a jaded workforce
○   focus efforts
○   reward outstanding performance
○   improve morale and motivation
○   encourage competition.

Prizes can be awarded in many different ways. The most obvious is for the highest sales figures over a given period (year, quarter, month and so on). But smaller prizes can also be used to great effect as incentives and teaching aids, especially if used creatively or humorously.

For instance, you might offer one prize for the most cold calls in the week, and another for the best sentence (of not more than 20 words!) starting with 'I love cold calling new clients because . . .'. Give a prize for the best 'close' of the week. Or use prizes to communicate disciplinary points: perhaps a 'prize' for the worst-dressed salesperson, or for the salesperson who makes the fewest company visits in a month.

Whatever the prize, the trick is to make it FUN! If you are offering a prize of a safari in Africa for the best performance all year, wear a pith helmet when you announce it, give people pictures of the scenery and hotel, bring in a stuffed elephant. Sell them the idea. The following is an example of how you can present something as humble (and inexpensive) as a dinner for two:

> 'The lights are low, music is tinkling softly in the background, the meal was delicious, superb even, and you stare into each other's eyes. The night is young. . . .. Yes, next Tuesday is Valentine's Day! And to help you celebrate in style, we are giving away – that's right, giving! – an all-expenses-paid dinner for two at the restaurant of your choice. All you have to do to qualify is arrange the largest number of appointments between now and February the 13th. So don't be shy! The evening of your dreams is only a few phone calls away!'

If you make competitions too serious, they can become demotivating: people resent being asked to jump through hoops on the off-chance of winning a bottle of wine, or even a safari in Africa. They will point out, quite rightly, that they work for their commission, not to win a prize.

If you expect your staff to put in extra effort, you must make the prize worth winning, and, if it is a big competition, you should offer second and third prizes: many people will think they haven't got a chance of coming first, and if you only offer one prize, they will not try. Also understand that some people will be more demotivated by the risk of failure than they will be motivated by the chance of winning. Some won't want to take part in any meaningful way. If these people are senior members of your team, you may want to remonstrate with them in private, but sometimes you *can* only lead a horse to water . . ..

While a competition is in progress, keep your staff informed – often salespeople lose track of their own performance. Sometimes they can be surprised to discover they have a chance of winning and this will inspire them to try that little bit harder. Publish daily or weekly figures showing everyone's position. Offer encouragement but be careful not to demotivate or humiliate.

Above all, whenever you run a competition, publish all rules in full. This avoids numerous rankles and possible ill will. The following are some guidelines:

O Define the precise criteria on which the competition will be judged (largest number of confirmed sales, or greatest cash value of confirmed sales – what does 'confirmed' mean?).
O State the exact date and time when the competition starts and ends.
O All disputes to be decided by you, and your word to be final.
O Any 'cheating' or 'figure-massaging' (in your opinion) immediately disqualifies.
O In the event of a draw, state how will you decide the final winner.

And finally, always be tactful when you award prizes: applaud the winner, but be careful to avoid making the runners-up feel like also-rans.

IDEAS FOR PRIZES

Competitions and prizes offer numerous opportunities for innovation and novelty. Here are some ideas.

Run a year-long competition with monthly or weekly winners accumulating points, which they can trade in at the end of the year for a prize of their choice. For instance, you could award 10 points to each week's highest performer, 5 points to the second highest, 2 points to the third. These points could then be exchanged as follows: 150 points win a weekend in Paris, 90 points a year's membership to a healthclub, 60 points a colour television or a video, 30 points a computer game, lawnmower or champagne dinner for two. Prizes are only awarded at the end of the year, thereby encouraging company loyalty and low staff turnover.

Choose exotic or unusual or luxury prizes. A week in Thailand or The Gambia sounds expensive and is exciting, but may cost your company less than a week in France. A hamper from Fortnum & Mason's is something few people have had and everyone would like to try. A monthly clothes allowance of £30 is a pleasant luxury, and may result in a better-dressed employee. A weekend trip to New York on Concorde will make anyone excited: on the last day of the competition ask everyone who might win to bring their passports and send the winner off to the airport in a taxi (and provide a glass of champagne for everyone!).

Introduce a monthly cup, or other such prize, awarded to the month's highest performer. No extra money comes with the cup, and at the end of the month it is passed on to the next winner. But salespeople rarely want to see it go and will try that little bit harder to hang on to it. Also the presence of the cup there on the person's desk for a month can do wonders for their self-esteem.

If you have a reasonably large sales force, establish a 'Wall of Fame' – a notice-board, or even better a hand-painted roll of honour on which are inscribed the names and sales figures of each quarter's highest achiever.

If you have more than one sales office, publicize performance results. How about a monthly sales news-sheet to swap figures, anecdotes and tips? And what about inter-office competitions?

And finally … **use prizes sparingly:** used too often, they lose their ability to excite.

8

EVALUATING THE SALES TEAM

Evaluation – the collection and analysis of information – is, in a sense, the starting-point of the sales manager's job. It identifies the strengths and weaknesses of your staff's performance, shows where improvements can and must be made, and measures the effectiveness of your efforts to boost performance.

As we shall see, for this evaluation to be meaningful, it must be based on information which is reliable, accurate and relevant, and must be conducted thoroughly and objectively. This chapter provides a complete and detailed introduction to all aspects of performance monitoring, statistical analysis and skills assessment. Subjects we cover include:

- What to assess
- How to measure performance
- Measuring quantitative data
- Analysing sales activities
- Assessing by volume
- Assessing by ratios
- Assessment – an example
- Measuring qualitative data
- Other forms of assessment
- Putting your assessment to work.

WHAT TO ASSESS

First of all, let's identify the range of figures and information you can collect. The following performance figures are essential to the sales process:

- Enquiries received
- Enquiries processed
- Canvass calls made to new and/or existing customers
- Meetings and/or demonstrations arranged
- Proposals presented
- Sales made (number, volume, value).

There is, of course, other information which can be just as important:

- New accounts won (number, name, details, market sector)
- Market sector (of sales made)

- Details of all lost accounts/sales (number, to whom, which market sector, size, type)
- Time between initial enquiry and eventual sale (that is, the turnaround time)
- Number of hours worked by each salesperson
- Amount of time spent on the phone
- Number of phone-calls made
- Miles travelled
- Size of expense account.

All of this information is factual, and is mainly numeric: it can be described as *quantitative*. We must also consider what sort of *qualitative* data we can assess:

- Time management, organization and efficiency
- Ability to produce paperwork, proposals and so on
- Ability to establish customer relationships
- Ability to sell
- Ability to present ideas and communicate
- Product, company and market knowledge
- Attitude and enthusiasm for work
- Relationship with other staff
- Relationship with management
- Ability to act on own initiative, implement change
- Ability to learn and adapt to change
- Future potential.

From these two lists we must now decide which factors will give us most insight into our staff's performance. In deciding what criteria will help you assess your staff most effectively, you should remember the following conditions:

- They must be *relevant* to the person's overall performance
- They must be *stable* (do not fluctuate wildly)
- They must clearly indicate the *difference* between good and bad performance
- They must be *measurable*.

Getting these key criteria right is vital, as how you assess your staff will inevitably affect your approach to most aspects of your work:

- What you look for when you recruit
- The emphasis of your training
- The emphasis of the salespeople's job descriptions
- The basis for promotion and discipline
- The ultimate success or failure of your sales team.

Take care therefore to select criteria which really are most relevant to your goals and your staff's performance. In most cases, you will want criteria which measure your staff's ability to:

- Make sales (this above all else)
- Perform the key aspects of their job
- Generate new business
- Establish good customer relations
- Present themselves and the company well.

Exactly which criteria you choose will depend on the nature of your business, but it is best to include both quantitative and qualitative values. Quantitative data are easier to measure and assess, but qualitative data often give better insights into a person's sales ability and potential. For instance, you may feel that the most important criteria are:

- Quantitative: numbers of new clients canvassed, meetings arranged, sales made.
- Qualitative: ability to sell, ability to communicate, positive attitude, ability to learn.

Once you have decided which activities and qualities you are going to assess (of course, you may decide to assess them *all*!), you must decide on the level of performance for each specific activity (that is, how well your salespeople should perform each one).

For quantitative data, such as the number of phone-calls made, or the volume of sales generated, your answer will be in terms of a number. For instance, staff should make 40 canvass calls a day; or staff should generate sales of £5 000 a month. Of course, you will only be able to arrive at realistic figures once you have started to monitor your staff's performance.

Qualitative criteria, on the other hand, such as 'the ability to sell' or 'the ability to create customer rapport', cannot be measured in this way. In fact the problem with judging whether someone has a quality like 'the ability to sell' is that our judgement can seem subjective and uncertain. For this reason, many sales managers do not try to assess these sorts of skills, but rely solely on their staff's performance figures. This is certainly simpler, but it can mean that salespeople whose figures are poor, but who have great potential, are not given the support or training they need to become successful. A better method is to take a quality like 'the ability to sell' and break it down into a list of activities which are less vague and are easier for you to assess. For instance, you might break 'the ability to sell' down as follows:

- Bright, friendly sales persona
- Establishes natural, positive rapport with customer
- Controls the sales conversation
- Gets the customer talking about their needs (and understands them)
- Interests the customer in our products
- Performs good presentations
- Appears professional
- Answers objections smoothly and satisfactorily
- Foresees and avoids problems
- Closes often and effectively
- Motivated to get results
- Good attention to detail.

The activities on this list are easier to measure and will help you encourage, discipline and train your staff.

Once you have decided on what you will assess and how well you expect your staff to perform each activity, you have what can be called a 'scale of values' – a scale against which you can measure the performance of each of your staff.

Bear in mind that this scale of values is to help you, not hinder you. You will probably want to revise your scale of values many times, in the light of experience and changing market conditions.

Once you have decided on your scale of values, you must communicate it effectively and clearly to your staff. There are five ways of doing this:

1. During the recruitment process (see Chapter 12 for details)
2. In the job description and sales manual (Chapter 4 deals with these topics)
3. In the sales meeting (for a full treatment of the sales meeting, see Chapter 6)
4. During goal-setting (see Chapter 5)
5. In everyday contact and discussion with the sales force (Chapter 6 on 'Communication' covers all aspects).

If your staff do not know what is expected of them, and are not constantly reminded, they will set themselves their own criteria and standards, which will usually be at variance with yours (for a reminder on this subject, see Chapter 4).

HOW TO MEASURE PERFORMANCE

In the rest of this chapter we review the various ways of measuring and interpreting quantitative and qualitative data. First of all, let's consider a basic and fundamental principle of assessing:

> For you to measure and assess your staff's performance effectively, your staff must believe in and trust the assessment process.

Staff can fail to believe in your assessment process if *they think*:

- You are judging them on the wrong criteria.
- You are interpreting the data incorrectly.
- The data is inaccurate.
- It is easy to mislead or hoodwink you.
- You only use the assessment as an opportunity to persecute them.

Whenever and however you are assessing staff, bear these points in mind. Always try to make your assessment process as objective and fair as possible. Let your staff know *what, why* and *how* you are assessing. Make sure your criteria are relevant to the sales process and conform with your staff's training and work practices (or else you will be assessing them on the wrong things). Don't use your assessment to discipline staff until it is firmly established and accepted: instead use it to praise and reward. Always praise people for making sales, no matter how good or bad various aspects of their performance may be.

The other issue which you will need to address is computerization. A computer can give you more information on your staff more easily and more quickly than any other form of measurement. The pros and cons of computerization are covered in Chapter 9.

In the rest of this chapter we will examine the following topics:

- Measuring quantitative data
- Analysing sales activities
- Assessing by volume
- Assessing by ratios
- Assessment – an example
- Measuring qualitative data
- Other forms of assessment
- Putting your assessment to work.

MEASURING QUANTITATIVE DATA

The best way of recording quantitative data is on a daily basis (see 'Monitoring performance' in Chapter 4). Wherever possible, the sales manager should take down the information required direct from the individual salesperson. This allows you to praise, encourage or question the salesperson on the spot, and keeps you in touch with the sales floor. Also, as salespeople know they have to give a daily account of their performance:

- they work harder, and
- they become less self-conscious of having their performance reviewed.

The disadvantages of this approach are:

○   it takes time, and
○   if the sales manager does not use this information constructively, staff will become resentful.

Typically, the sales manager will have a daily figure sheet something like the one shown in Table 8.1.

TABLE 8.1   DAILY FIGURE SHEET

Name	Canvass Calls	New enquiries	Meetings	Presentations	Proposals	Sales
David	30	7	1	0	0	0
Anwar	25	8	2	0	0	1
Geoffrey	35	3	2	1	1	0
Elizabeth	37	2	1	1	0	0
Anne	34	4	1	0	1	1

We will use these performance figures, and others concerning these five salespeople, to demonstrate how to assess sales activities in the following sections.

Analysing sales activities

There are two ways of analysing performance figures which we will consider in the next two sections: by *volume* and by *ratios*. For the best results, these two methods should be used in conjunction. Both of them are only accurate, however, if we base them in the right context. By context I mean:

○   each person's average performance
○   the sales team's average performance
○   any external factors to be taken into consideration
○   our own observations of each salesperson.

We can see this as soon as we consider the example of performance figures in the previous section.

On this day both David and Anwar handled more enquiries than anyone else – is this due to factors beyond their control (for example how the post was allocated) or to their efforts (for example better canvassing)? The two sales of the day should be understood in the context of the work which went into them: was Anwar's sale merely confirmed today, or did he spend all day working to agree the deal? Finally, Elizabeth's figures seem quite low, but you might know from observation that she spent all day working hard and was 'unlucky' in not achieving more quantifiable results.

In all of these instances, anyone basing an assessment on the sales figures alone would be jumping to inaccurate conclusions.

Assessing by volume

Assessing by volume is the simplest form of assessment. It involves assessing each person according to the volume or quantity of their performance figures (for example, the bigger the number of canvass calls, the better). We have already seen that, depending on the context, this form of assessment can be inaccurate. We can make it more accurate, however, by assessing a salesperson's daily figures in relation to their *average* figures.

When we examine the salespeople's averages over a three-month period, we are able to get a clearer idea of each person's true output:

TABLE 8.2 QUARTERLY FIGURE SHEET

Name	Canvass Calls	New enquiries	Meetings	Presentations	Proposals	Sales
David	31/day	3/day	4/week	2/week	1.5/week	3/mth
Anwar	22/day	8/day	7/week	5/week	3.5/week	8/mth
Geoffrey	33/day	3/day	8/week	5/week	3/week	5/mth
Elizabeth	40/day	5/day	5/week	1/week	1/week	3/mth
Anne	34/day	3/day	6/week	3/week	2/week	4/mth
Average	32/day	4.4/day	6/week	3.2/week	2.2/week	4.6/mth

In addition to this, it is probably best to assess your staff according to their *weekly* figures. This will give you an immediate and accurate insight into each person's current level of work, while avoiding the inconsistencies of daily results.

Lists of averages should be regularly updated. This will enable you to become aware of trends and changes as they occur (and if necessary, correct them). However, for our assessments to be really informative, we will need to use the other method of assessment we mentioned earlier: assessment by ratios.

Assessing by ratios

Assessing performance figures by their ratios can throw a different light on our staff's performance and helps us gain a clearer picture of their strengths and weaknesses. Here are the quarterly figures from the last section re-calculated as *monthly* ratios:

TABLE 8.3 MONTHLY RATIOS

Name	Calls: Enquiries	Enquiries: Meetings	Meetings: Presentations	Presentations: Proposals	Proposals: Sales
David	10:1	3.8:1	2:1	1.3:1	2.2:1
Anwar	2.8:1	5.7:1	1.4:1	1.4:1	1.9:1
Geoffrey	11:1	1.9:1	1.6:1	1.7:1	2.6:1
Elizabeth	8:1	5:1	5:1	1:1	1.4:1
Anne	11:1	2.5:1	2:1	1.5:1	2.2:1
Average	7.3:1	3.7:1	1.9:1	1.5:1	2.1:1

By using the two forms of assessment together (assessing by volume and by ratios) we can draw conclusions about our staff's performance and ability which are valuable and reasonably accurate. Even these conclusions must be used only as the starting-point of our assessment, not the final word.

Assessment – an example

What follows is an assessment by volume and by ratios of the sample performance figures we have been using. In particular, this example shows how to use ratio-assessment effectively.

Anwar: Anwar is your most successful salesperson, and makes an average of 8 sales a month. What is most remarkable about his performance is the number of enquiries he generates from canvassing (8 a day, as opposed to an average for the others of only 3.5). How is he managing this? Is it through superior canvassing techniques (in which case can these be taught to the others?) or is he receiving leads from other sources? Or does he merely count enquiries more readily (or more hastily) than the others? Would this explain why he converts fewer enquiries into meetings than other staff (a ratio of only 5.7:1) – could this be improved? These questions can only be answered by your *observation, judgement*, and *discussion* with Anwar. You must also ask why Anwar makes significantly fewer canvass calls a day than the others – is this because he spends more time on each one, or could he generate even more leads by making more canvass calls?

Anwar is also very successful at converting meetings into full presentations (the best ratio in the team). Again, you should assess how he conducts his meetings and whether there are lessons to be learned. Interestingly, Anwar's ratios of converting presentations into requests for proposals, and converting proposals into sales, are only average, so he is probably not doing anything better at these stages than the other staff: he is simply able to process *more* of these than the others.

David: David is in comparison one of your poorest performers. The ratios do not point to any glaring differences with the others: most of his figures are more or less average. They suggest a mediocre performer who may not be capable of significant improvement in any one area.

Geoffrey: Geoffrey, however, has several distinct strong points: he converts enquiries into meetings very well (his ratio of 1.9:1 is the best), and does very well at turning meetings into presentations. His end-results are also good (5 sales/month). His main problem is turning proposals into sales (ratio of 2.6:1 is the worst). How can you interpret this? Are Geoffrey's proposals as well-written and well-presented as, for instance, Elizabeth's? Or does the cause lie elsewhere? Perhaps Geoffrey forces proposals on customers who are not interested, or perhaps he fails to understand his customers' needs, so his proposals are wide of the mark? Geoffrey's canvassing is also not good (11 calls for 1 lead), although, unlike Anwar, this could be because he does not count anything as an 'enquiry' unless it is particularly hopeful – this would provide a different interpretation of his excellent Enquiries:Meetings ratio.

Elizabeth: Elizabeth's canvassing skills and volume are excellent. So are her ratios for Presentations:Proposals and Proposals:Sales. But her ratio of Enquiries:Meetings is poor and her ability to turn Meetings into Presentations is disastrous. If you can discover what her weakness is (and correct it), you might turn Elizabeth into a really high performer.

Anne: Anne is a good, average performer. Her figures and ratios suggest she is competent in all areas, although her canvassing could be improved: this would probably feed through into better sales figures.

Overall: The assessor must also ask whether he or she is satisfied with the team's overall performance. Is the total volume of sales acceptable? Does the team generate enough new enquiries as a whole? Are 4.4 enquiries a day sufficient to keep each salesperson fully occupied? Would performance improve if each salesperson had more enquiries and was not under such pressure to convert each one into a meeting?

The above is a good example of how an assessment forms the start of your evaluation, not the finishing-point: you should correlate whatever the figures suggest with your own observations, judgement and discussion with the people concerned.

MEASURING QUALITATIVE DATA

Unlike quantitative data, qualitative information depends much more on your personal *opinion* of your salespeople's performance. For this reason, you need to make a conscious effort to assess your salespeople as fairly and objectively as possible or else the value of your assessment will be extremely limited. Basic guidelines for a fair assessment follow.

Establish in advance the criteria you wish to use

Refer back to the list of qualities and skills and decide which ones are relevant to your assessment – and apply them to all staff. As we have seen, if your criteria are vague they will be more difficult to assess. Therefore break down criteria into smaller units which are easier to measure.

Define good and bad performance in advance

Wherever possible, create written definitions of each of your criteria. For instance, 'Good canvassing technique' might be defined as: 'Bright, friendly voice. Handles reception well. Presents enthusiastically to client. Overcomes initial resistance. Closes effectively.' When observing your staff canvassing, refer each person's performance to this list. This prevents your overall impression of the salesperson from unduly colouring your judgement.

Establish a friendly atmosphere

The salesperson must feel you are there to help and praise, not to obstruct and criticize.

Assess regularly

The more often you assess, the more natural your staff will be, and the greater the insights you will gain.

Assess to improve

Conduct assessments to help your staff improve. Whenever you observe a salesperson making a mistake or failing to achieve their objective (for example, failing to win a meeting or make a sale), ask yourself 'How could they have done this better? What could they do to succeed?' This sort of question helps you interpret your observations, and enables you to advise and support your staff. By identifying how your staff need to improve, you can expose the root causes of their problems.

Recording your assessment

There are several different methods of recording your assessment. All have their merits.
Marks on a scale: Grade each skill on a scale of 1 to 5 or 1 to 7. This tends to appear objective, but it can lend your assessment a pseudo-scientific air.
Relate each assessment to the average: Assess each skill as 'average', 'above average', 'below average'. This begs the question of whether 'average' is good enough, but at least it helps you identify particularly good and poor performance.
Written report: A short two- or three-line assessment of each skill. This takes longer, but is more accurate and avoids any spurious 'grading' of staff. Include suggestions for improvement.

OTHER FORMS OF ASSESSMENT

We have now reviewed the main ways of assessing your staff in the field. However, there are other valuable approaches which can help you gauge your staff's performance, attitude and potential. We shall consider the following two:

○ Self-assessment
○ Psychometric testing.

SELF-ASSESSMENT

A novel and surprisingly effective method is to ask your staff to assess themselves. If this is done in a positive, responsible atmosphere, you may be surprised at some of the perceptions and self-criticisms your staff produce. There are many attractions in this technique for you:

○ It provides you with a different perspective.
○ Staff are more likely to believe in it.
○ It provides the basis for an interesting discussion about the person's performance.
○ If staff criticize themselves, they are demonstrating some commitment to improving themselves.

Self-assessment works best if staff are provided with forms they can fill in, giving them a structure and forcing them to review their whole work record. These assessments should be conducted regularly, but not too often (say once every three or six months). Self-assessment does not work when staff do not take it seriously or give false and misleading answers. A typical self-assessment form is given in Figure 8.1.

Self-assessments need to be interpreted in a friendly, constructive manner with the person concerned. One of the most important questions to ask is always 'Why?' 'Why do you think you performed as you did?' 'Why do you think your best skill is canvassing?'

Another revealing form of self-assessment is to ask your staff to list the various sales activities in order of preference – and then again in order of importance.

PSYCHOMETRIC TESTING

Gaining popularity throughout industry, psychometric testing seeks to analyse people's personalities and from this assess their strengths, weaknesses, motivational needs and potential. For these tests to produce reliable information they must be conducted and analysed by trained personnel. The insights they provide can be invaluable, and can help managers understand and respond to their staff. The only word of caution: staff can be very distrustful of such methods, and can feel betrayed and angry if they think you set more store by a psychometric report than by your own relationship with them. Psychometric tests should always be in addition to, not in place of, personal assessments.

PUTTING YOUR ASSESSMENT TO WORK

You should now be able to combine your personal observation of each salesperson's skills and qualities with the suggestions and implications of your statistical analysis. What does this tell you about each salesperson? Where do you see their strengths and weaknesses? Do you think the implications of your statistical analysis are borne out on the sales floor? Or do the problems lie elsewhere? Your assessment can now be used in a number of ways.

TO SET GOALS AND DISCUSS PERFORMANCE

Do not assess your staff if you are not prepared to discuss your findings with them. Ask for their feedback, and explanations. Praise and encourage where due. Unless you conduct regular and credible assessments of your staff, you cannot set meaningful goals and

FIGURE 8.1 STAFF SELF-ASSESSMENT FORM

Name ....

How would you rate your overall performance in the last 3 months?

In the last 3 months, what do you think your main achievements have been in terms of improving your work?

Are there any areas you are not happy with, or in which you have not made progress?

Looking at the following aspects of your job, how would you rate your performance in each one:
- Canvassing:
- Handling new enquiries:
- Conducting the sales meeting:
- Preparing proposals:
- Making the final presentation:
- Objection-handling:
- Closing:
- Appearance:
- Phonework:
- Product knowledge:

Which do you feel are your particular strengths?

Which do you feel are your particular weaknesses?

Where would you like to receive additional training?

Please enter your sales figures for the last 3 months:
Month 1:
Month 2:
Month 3:
How would you assess this performance?

Do you think you could have done better, or are you basically happy with your final result?

How do you expect to perform in the next 3 months?

How would you like to see yourself progressing in the next year?

What would you particularly like to get out of your work in the coming months?

standards of performance – nor can you see if those goals are achieved. See Chapter 5 for full details of reviews and goal-setting.

TO DEVELOP A TRAINING PROGRAMME

Assessment should show who needs training, and in what. It might also suggest which members of your staff might have something to teach the others. For a full treatment of this, refer to the companion volume to this book, *Training the Sales Team*, which contains the material for 12 complete training courses.

TO IDENTIFY YOUR MAIN PRIORITIES

What do your findings identify as key areas of concern? Should your staff be making more canvass calls, or spending more hours in the office? Should they be improving the quality of their proposals, or should you be helping them overcome more objections?

Sometimes assessments can produce startling results. One sales manager discovered that his staff only chased 11 per cent of new sales enquiries, meaning that a potential 89 per cent of new business was being ignored. By enforcing more thorough enquiry handling, sales were boosted by 25 per cent in a six-month period.

Generally speaking, any figure which is out of the ordinary should be investigated: typically they indicate areas where a salesperson is weak or just downright lazy! Assessments often show that some salespeople make less than half the number of client service calls that their colleagues do, or send out only a fraction of the letters, brochures and so on. These are factors you can correct, usually through discipline. In these cases never be afraid to confront the culprits with the hard facts and figures.

SUMMARY

By conducting regular, systematic assessments you will become more aware of the detail of your staff's performance and the particular steps that are needed to improve and correct it. Assessing staff will bring more structure to your work, as well as your staff's, and gives the team a framework within which they can operate. Regular assessments also make salespeople more aware of their own performance and encourage the process of self-assessment and self-improvement that is so valuable in a successful salesperson.

9
ADMINISTRATION AND ORGANIZATION

❖

In this chapter 'administration' refers to the whole process of sales office support: paperwork, secretarial support, figure-taking, order-processing. Every sales manager knows that efficient, effective administration is essential to a well-run and successful sales team. Managers also know that too much administration can choke the sales process and can make you and your staff slaves to paperwork and bureaucracy. This chapter will help you get the best from your administration – while avoiding the worst. It covers the following subjects:

○ Assessing your administration
○ Planning improvements
○ How to improve administration
○ Keeping and using records
○ Computerization.

ASSESSING YOUR ADMINISTRATION

These are questions to ask yourself:

❖ What information does my current administration give me? How accurate is it? Do I use it all? Is there any other information I could use? Refer to Chapter 8 for examples of the sort of information you could be receiving.

❖ Do I spend too long collecting information?

❖ Is there any administrative activity I do which is time-consuming? Could it be more effectively performed by someone else?

❖ Does my current administration provide me with suitable support? Do I have effective and efficient systems set up for processing letters, producing proposals, taking phone-calls, recording messages, notifying me of staff's reviews, and so on?

❖ What is the quality and speed of administrative support I and my staff receive? Is it good enough?

These are questions to ask your staff (and yourself):

❖ What aspects of the current administration do you find most helpful? (Letter-writing, document-processing, customer information and so on.)

❖ What aspects do you find unhelpful – or would like to see improved? (Figure-taking, form-filling, length of time for letters to get typed.)

❖ What is the quality of customer and competitor information currently available? How quickly and easily can it be accessed? Is it up-to-date and accurate?

When these questions were asked at one company, one of the complaints the salespeople made was that it took the office staff (and management!) too long to process incoming mail in the morning. This meant that the sales staff did not receive enquiry letters until after 10.30 am, whereas several of their competitors had them (and could respond to them) an hour earlier. As with many complaints, what was at issue was not the difference this made to sales figures, but the degree of frustration the sales force experienced.

PLANNING IMPROVEMENTS

Once you have completed your assessment (in whatever detail is appropriate to the scale of your organization), you might decide to make improvements. The scope and extent of these will obviously depend on the resources of your administration team and your control over it. As a general rule, the sales department's access to administration and secretarial support should be second only to the executive board's. Unfortunately this is not always the case.

A good way of planning improvements to your administration is to draw up a complete description of all your administrative functions: those you do yourself (such as figure-taking), those done by other salespeople, those done by office support staff. Assess the quality of each of these functions, and any improvements you would like to see. Then add to the list any administrative tasks you want to introduce. Points to bear in mind are:

○ Of all these activities, which are unnecessary, or can be transferred to someone else whose time is less valuable, or more available?

○ Now, what sort of improvement do you want? A qualitative improvement (such as 'faster typing times' or 'less time spent making coffee')? Or a totally new practice introduced (such as monitoring enquiries, or making one secretary responsible for typing all sales letters)?

○ Finally, as in planning all management tasks, what is most important? What will reap greatest benefits? What are your priorities?

Your assessment and implementation chart may look something like Table 9.1.

TABLE 9.1   ASSESSMENT AND IMPLEMENTATION CHART

Activity	Assessment	Improvement	Priority
Done by me:			
Record all daily sales	Vital to stay in touch, but takes 30 minutes each day	Aim to combine this with other activities	
Read proposals to key accounts	Someone needs to read them, but time-consuming	Could team leaders do this?	
Read all letters received	Unnecessary	Secretaries to only pass me problem letters	
Prepare all corporate proposals	Necessary, but time-consuming	Can the layout and text of proposals be standardized?	
Prepare all product literature	Necessary	None obvious	

TABLE 9.1 (CONTINUED)

Activity	Assessment	Improvement	Priority
Done by sales force:			
Report all sales	Vital, though staff are sometimes lax	Make team leaders responsible for ensuring staff report?	
Write letters to current accounts	Necessary, though often takes up valuable time	Designate slack times (for example 12 to 1 o'clock) for writing. Standardize letters	
Prepare proposals	Essential, but time-consuming	Investigate standardizing proposals. Designate time	
Store all customer data	Necessary, but wastes time	A secretary to do this instead	
By admin. department:			
Type all letters	Good quality, though takes long time for letters to be processed	Introduce system of prioritization, so key letters are typed immediately	
Open and log all incoming post	Time-consuming (takes 4 secretaries 1 hour), and delays sales staff	Is this necessary? Perhaps we can only log new enquiries. How can we ensure they are followed up?	
Type all proposals	Sales staff can have problems getting the layout they desire. Also takes time	Designate one secretary full-time. Agree corporate layout style. Standardize as much as possible. Prioritize	
Perform all filing	Sometimes only done once a week. Not always accurate	Give responsibility to one person. Demand filing done every day. Check up	
Find data on customers	Good. Quick (providing it's been filed)	None necessary	

New activities to be introduced	How to introduce	Benefit	
By myself:			
Collecting more performance data (see Chapter 8)	Can be combined with taking daily sales figures	Will be able to evaluate staff's efficiency and effectiveness	
Reviewing new accounts with staff	Staff to report these as soon as they happen	I can praise straight away, I can understand how new accounts are won, and gauge their potential	
By sales force:			
Reporting more detailed activity figures each day	As part of daily figures	Will enable me to assess performance, and will make staff more aware	
Keeping details of enquiries processed	Need new form which must be handed in each week	Ensure more enquiries are followed up	
By admin. department:			
Check enquiries processed against list of enquiries by post	Collect lists from staff, showing enquiries processed, and names of those still outstanding	Saves me time. Enables me to concentrate on trouble spots	

Now, before committing yourself to any course of action, consult with the administration staff and your own staff: what improvements can they suggest? Do they think your ideas are practicable and beneficial? Are your admin. department able to implement your changes with their current resources?

HOW TO IMPROVE ADMINISTRATION

The example in the last section highlights many of the key techniques of improving administrative functions:

- Standardization
- Delegation
- Specialization
- Prioritization
- Time allocation
- Deadlines
- Structure system.

We will consider these briefly.

STANDARDIZATION

Draw up a range of standard letters which will cope with virtually all business situations, and which your secretaries can then personalize as your staff wish. You can have standard letters covering the following: responses to general enquiries; responses to specific enquiries (for example, one letter for customers interested in prices, one for build-quality, one for customer service and so on); letters confirming meetings, telephone conversations, demonstrations and so on; letters acknowledging complaints; letters confirming sales and orders; letters for customers who are uncontactable.

All proposals should also be standardized as much as possible, and their layouts confirmed with admin.

As well as saving your secretaries and your staff time, standard formats also improve and maintain the quality of your department's written output: not all your salespeople will be natural letter-writers.

DELEGATION

If certain tasks disrupt your working day and are non-essential, delegate them. Always retain some sort of quality control, and make sure the person concerned is adequately recompensed – not necessarily financially, but with thanks, and responsibility.

SPECIALIZATION

Tasks will be performed more quickly and with more care if your administrative staff specialize: for instance, it is easier to teach one secretary how to produce professional reports, than to teach six. Particularly boring and monotonous tasks should be shared.

PRIORITIZATION

If you cannot improve the efficiency of a system, you can at least ensure that important tasks are performed first. All proposals should be prioritized by you wherever appropriate, and both your sales and admin. staff should know which tasks should take priority.

TIME ALLOCATION

Tasks are done more quickly if specific times are set aside for them with no disruptions. If you set strict times for certain tasks, this also stops them taking longer than they ought and sprawling over into other parts of the day.

DEADLINES

You should also obtain (or agree) with admin. the deadlines for paperwork and typing. This is the time admin. must receive paperwork by, if they are to guarantee to process it by the end of work. This prevents admin. making excuses, and puts the onus back on the salespeople to organize themselves.

STRUCTURED SYSTEM

Your staff should work in a structured, organized environment, geared towards making sales. The whole order-taking process should be as smooth and structured as possible. It should require the minimum amount of paperwork and time-wasting. It should also be strictly adhered to. For further details on structuring your staff's day, see Chapter 4.

KEEPING AND USING RECORDS

Detailed accurate records are necessary if you are to manage your staff effectively. At the same time you don't want to spend all day either writing information down or looking it up (a computerized sales system can help you avoid this). The following is the essential minimum information on each of your staff:

Personal details
- Standard personal history: date of birth, education, and so on.
- The date the person joined the company (and the reason why, if known).
- Details of all reviews, promotions, salary awards, plus details of any discussions about that person's ambitions, likes, dislikes and so on.
- Details of any complaints and how they were resolved.
- Details of all commission and earnings.

Work details
- Each person's performance figures (see Chapter 8 for full information on this).
- Details of all sales (what, to whom, when).
- Notes on sales which were lost.
- Sales forecast for the current sales period.

PUTTING YOUR RECORDS TO WORK

On a day-to-day basis, it is the second category of information (on work) which will be invaluable.

If you take daily sales figures in person, ask your staff to explain them (for example, why so many effective phone calls? Why so few appointments?) Help them to understand the reasons for their results. Then agree with them what they will do the next day (continue or change tactics, concentrate on getting more appointments and so on). Make a note of it. The next day use this as your introduction to their work. (How are they finding things? Have they achieved more appointments? Why not?) This helps keep the person focused on an objective, and helps you keep on top of what they are doing.

On a weekly or fortnightly basis, go through all of your staff's current enquiries, leads, meetings, proposals, outstanding offers and so on. For each meeting and proposal you should ask for a full status report and discuss with the salesperson the likelihood of the lead/enquiry/meeting turning into a sale. What problems have they had? What problems can they foresee? What advice or encouragement can you offer?

By conducting such regular reviews of your staff's work-in-progress (note this is not goal-setting), you will keep yourself abreast of each and every development. You will also prevent your staff from missing or losing opportunities, and will provide them with a useful fillip if necessary. This sort of review need not be conducted in private, but can be done on the sales floor. Your tone should not be aggressive or highly critical, though it should be thorough, and you should not let yourself be fobbed off with excuses.

If your staff spend most of the day on client sites, monitoring their performance can be more difficult, although, if anything, more important. Many companies solve this difficulty by means of portable computers, on which salespeople record sales, visits and so on. However, this is not always possible – or affordable. Here is a suggested framework:

- Salespeople should give you a list of scheduled visits and so on for your approval, together with notes on their expectations: are they routine, in response to an enquiry?
- Salespeople phone in results every evening: sales, types of products sold, rejections, further appointments arranged.
- You review performance with the person there and then and discuss the calls scheduled for tomorrow.

COMPUTERIZATION

Many of the functions we have considered in the last two chapters (figure-taking, performance-monitoring, letter-writing, enquiry-processing) can be more effectively performed by computer. Computer systems are not always affordable or available to every sales manager, but this section briefly considers some of their pros and cons and suggests ways in which they can be used to maximum effect.

USING COMPUTERS TO RECORD AND ANALYSE SALES ACTIVITIES

Computerization has revolutionized the amount and accuracy of data which can be captured and processed. A sophisticated sales support system will do far more than just record the number of sales made. It will provide full information on:

- All clients (their size, market, interest)
- All client contact (when they were last contacted, by whom, with what result, their current status)
- All letters and proposals sent
- All meetings attended
- All complaints, queries and so on.

Once you have this information on your database, you can use computers to:

- Analyse market trends
- Group together useful pieces of client information
- Identify the types and locations of your best potential customers
- Automatically and regularly mailshot potential customers.

Also remember that, unlike paper records, computer records are harder to lose and easier to update.

USING COMPUTERS TO PLAN AND MONITOR SALES ACTIVITIES

As well as recording information, computers can also be used to help your staff organize themselves and work more efficiently. For instance, they can provide you and your staff with:

- A list of scheduled canvass calls each day (plus call-backs from the day/s before)
- A list of enquiries not followed up
- A list of outstanding proposals, meetings and so on
- An analysis of the time-scales involved (turnaround times)
- Details of all messages taken.

USING COMPUTERS TO IMPROVE PAPERWORK

Standard software packages and laser printers enable you to produce a previously unattainable quality of paperwork more quickly and easily than ever before:

- The facility to personalize standard letters acknowledging enquiries, confirming details of meetings, quotations and so on
- The facility to process sales and orders quickly and efficiently
- The facility to mailshot customers quickly and with personalized letters.

Also the reliability and efficiency of computer systems will improve your staff's morale and pride in their work – providing they *are* reliable and efficient!

WHAT ARE THE DRAWBACKS?

In general the use of computer systems is justified in sales. The advantages and applications of computer systems listed above are only a small sample of the ways computers can benefit you and help improve sales performance. Companies who have installed computer systems have seen average improvements of over 10 per cent in the first quarter, and over 20 per cent in the second. It is only fair to mention some of the potential drawbacks computerization can bring:

- Staff must be shown the positive benefits of the computer system (such as speed, less paperwork, more sales) and not just the negative ones (greater accountability, more management control).
- You must review the ease with which data can be entered on the system: too easy and your database can become corrupt; too difficult and no one will bother.
- Introducing and implementing a new computer system while ensuring continuity and motivation is a difficult management task and needs careful and patient planning.
- Sales will almost always improve with the help of a good computer system, but management should not demand improvements straight away: this can lead to resentment.
- Computer systems cannot simply be added on to the salesperson's daily work: it means he or she has more work to do, not less. The computer should be used to replace the administrative tasks the salesperson already has to do.
- New computer systems often require extensive data entry. You will need to make allowances for this, probably by hiring temporary support staff to help.

SUMMARY

Administration is necessary for the smooth running of the sales team and for the optimization of your resources. Be prepared to spend time and money improving your administration. Any improvements must be judged against your staff's morale, ease of working and end-results. Administration should never stand in the way of sales.

10

CUSTOMER SERVICE

Sales is the process of providing our customers with solutions to their needs. It follows that the best way of boosting sales performance long-term is by improving the quality of customer service. This chapter examines some of the simple ways stronger, more lasting customer relationships can be achieved and used to increase results. The subjects it covers are as follows:

- Benefits of customer service
- Developing customer service
- Targeting customers
- The customer service questionnaire
- Gaining referrals
- After-sales service
- Handling complaints
- Conclusion: looking to the future.

BENEFITS OF CUSTOMER SERVICE

Let's start by summarizing the main benefits that come from good customer relations:

- The more you understand your customers' needs, the more effectively you will sell to them.
- Once your customers are aware of your understanding, they will trust you more and want to do more business with you.
- You will create a spirit of partnership between you and your customers.
- You are less likely to lose customers to competitors.
- Customers will involve you in their plans and developments.
- Customers will refer business to you.

Take these benefits as your aims. Constantly review your working practices and sales approaches in the light of these aims.

DEVELOPING CUSTOMER SERVICE

This section reviews simple ways of developing and improving customer service. Specific approaches examined are:

- Establishing a rota
- How effective are your customer calls?
- Customer specialization
- Better titles
- Create more contact time

ESTABLISHING A ROTA

How often your staff call your customers will depend on your market and type of business. However, it should be as regular and frequent as possible. Identify the shortest decision-making period relevant to your product and aim to ring on that basis. For many businesses this may mean telephoning your customers once a month, because they will have monthly meetings when they review budget, cash flow, outstanding business and so on. In other companies a quarterly cycle might be more appropriate; in still others weekly. In some markets, a regular visit, not a telephone call, is more effective, but increasingly companies are replacing visits with telemarketing. Telemarketing (telephone canvassing) is quicker, costs less, and enables your staff to concentrate on those leads which look most promising. Most customers prefer telemarketing as it is less disruptive and time-consuming than a visit.

Once you have decided how often your regular customers should be called, you need to establish the administrative system to ensure it. Work out how many clients each salesperson must contact each day and allocate accordingly. With a computer this is easy, as your staff can be given a list of clients to contact each morning, and if they fail to make the calls, the names are automatically added to their list for the next morning. However, customer service cards can be an effective substitute.

HOW EFFECTIVE ARE YOUR CUSTOMER CALLS?

Salespeople should use customer calls to develop long-term relationships and build mutual understanding. To help them do this, staff should be provided with customer call record sheets (or equivalent computer facilities) which make them record the following after each call:

- Contact spoken to
- What happened? What was discussed?
- What problems, needs or future developments were identified?
- What action is there to be taken? (What action agreed with the client?)
- What sales were made (if relevant)?
- Objectives for the next call/visit
- Date (and time) for next call/visit.

This quality of record makes each service call part of an ongoing process which leads naturally towards the next sale. Your salesperson will develop rapport with the customer and gain a greater understanding of how to present your products. The customers will feel your calls are *relevant*.

These records should be available for you to monitor your staff's performance, offer them advice, and forecast sales.

CUSTOMER SPECIALIZATION

Often salespeople are given geographical territories to work. This has attractions if their job involves extensive travelling, but is it always for the best? If you are selling goods or services to different types of companies, it might be more effective to allocate your sales force according to *vertical markets* (for example, one person for engineering companies, one for distributors, one for support services). This enables your staff to gain expert knowledge in their area: they get to know all the players in the market (big and small), they gain understanding of their customers' business, and learn what issues are current.

Wherever possible, avoid more than one salesperson talking to a client: it confuses the client and can lead to your salespeople actually selling against each other.

BETTER TITLES

Customers like to feel they are dealing with someone important. Can you call your experienced salespeople regional sales managers even if they work on their own? Or simply managers? Perhaps the person handling serious customer complaints can be called the director of customer care.

CREATE MORE CONTACT TIME

How can you reorganize your salespeople's days to give them more time with their customers? Can you stipulate that the first visit of the day must be at 9.00 am (or earlier) and the last not before 4.30? Don't encourage long, dreary meetings: train staff to conduct short, bright and effective visits, 30 minutes to 1 hour long. Review your salespeople's itineraries – how efficient are they?

TARGETING CUSTOMERS

Not all customers and potential customers are of equal value to you. Make sure that the customers who are most important are provided with the best service. Unfortunately, in many companies all customers are treated the same, whereas salespeople should be spending most time with the customer who is most likely to buy. Start by assessing all those companies or individuals who have bought from you.

If you are making one-off sales, you will want to analyse this list to find out what are the qualities or needs these customers had in common. They may fall into more than one type, so avoid too simplistic an analysis, but this will help you predict who your future customers are most likely to be.

If repeat business is of value to you, obviously this list of previous customers represents your most valuable asset. In addition to identifying their common traits, introduce an 'elite customer service plan' to make sure these customers stay sold on your products and buy them in the future.

You are now in a position to classify your customer database as follows:

A All those customers who have bought, may buy again and have an identifiable set of 'prime customer' qualities.
B All those customers who have the same (or almost the same) qualities and needs as Group A, but who have not yet bought.
C Other companies/individuals who might buy your products.

In some markets you might change this classification. For instance you might restrict the A group to only those companies who place frequent orders. Or you might split the B group into two – one for potential customers who match the profile of the A group, and one for companies who buy your type of product extensively but from your competitors.

Once you have decided on your classification (and agreed it with your staff), you must decide how to most effectively serve and exploit your A and B categories (again, you should discuss this with your staff). Here are some suggestions:

- Clients who are 'frequent purchasers' should be rung more frequently than average. For instance, if you normally ring clients once a month, you might ring these every two weeks.
- C-group clients should still be rung, but on a less frequent and time-consuming basis (perhaps once every two or three months).
- A-group customers should be regularly visited, they should be kept abreast of future product developments (and consulted), and they should be made to feel important. If your telephone lines are often busy, can A-group customers be given an 'executive service number' to ring?
- A-group customers should be given one steady contact who knows them personally. If this person is unavailable, can you help them yourself, or can you appoint an office support person for this function?
- Ask your staff to focus on certain B-group clients every month: how can they turn them into A-group clients? If staff know these companies are the ones most likely to buy, they will feel more confident and motivated in their efforts. It is worth aiming specific promotional offers at these companies.
- Any complaints from an A-group customer should be given top priority and every effort made to ensure that you retain their loyalty. (See the section on 'Handling complaints' later in this chapter.)
- If you discover an A-group customer buying from another source, you must respond immediately. Find out, politely, why your customer bought from elsewhere: is this due to a deficiency in your products or because your customer was not aware of your full product range? Would the customer consider placing other similar orders with you? Have you done anything (or failed to do something) which has soured your relationship? What can you do to prevent this happening again?
- As well as contacting A-group customers personally, keep in touch by regular mailshots, newsletters, free market surveys and the like. Anything to keep them interested, and if possible, grateful.
- All customers should receive regular after-sales service calls.
- Review your knowledge of your A- and B-group customers: how much do you really know? Do you have the names of all the key decision-makers, or are there other people your contacts can introduce you to? Do you know how your customer's business operates? What is important to them? How will their business develop?
- Many companies build long-term relationships with their prime customers by involving them in the research and design of future products, and by asking how they would like to see products or services developed. If you do not do this already, consider introducing it as soon as possible. Your salespeople should be asking all their clients about possible improvements and future needs all the time.
- Pamper and treat your A-group customers (and perhaps your best B-group customers). Corporate entertainment does not have to be expensive and can be vital in building company loyalty. A few obvious points: don't let corporate entertainment degenerate into an excuse for excessive drinking (this can actually lose customers); ensure that your salespeople are also present (and treated as equals by yourself); often activities (a day spent go-kart racing or yachting) can be more memorable and build customer loyalty – only ensure your activities will not embarrass or discomfort your customers.

THE CUSTOMER SERVICE QUESTIONNAIRE

If you want to improve the quality of service you provide, you have first to be aware of how your company is perceived by your customers. Are you in danger of losing business to your competitors or are your customers planning to buy less – or more? How can you increase the profile of your company?

One of the best ways of answering these questions is through a customer service questionnaire. Used properly, a customer service questionnaire is one of the most effective ways of developing strong customer relationships – and boosting sales.

As with all good ideas, this should be launched at a sales meeting. Devise, with your staff, a set of questions about your company, your service, and the market. Then agree with your staff to go through the questionnaire with your A- and B-group customers (or you may want to target your current customers or those businesses you would like to 'convert').

Each salesperson is to explain the questionnaire to the customer in the following terms: 'As you know, Mr Jones, we are always trying to improve the service we can offer you. To help us find out how we can do this, we are conducting a survey of our customers (and potential customers). Can I ask you a few questions?'

Most customers will be delighted to oblige. Of course the aims of the questionnaire may vary, but they will usually be:

○ To present your company in a favourable light.
○ To make the customer more aware of your goods, services and so on.
○ To encourage your customer to make more use of your services.
○ To build a closer relationship.
○ To find out how you could improve.
○ To find out how your customer perceives your company.
○ To find out what your customer thinks of your competition.

FIGURE 10.1   CUSTOMER SERVICE QUESTIONNAIRE

Customer Company Name ....

        Contact ....   Date ....

1   What do you look for in a company operating in our market? What are the most important qualities, aspects of service and so on?

2   Do you think our company meets these standards?

3   What do you think the main benefits of our service/products are to you?

4   Is that why you use us? (If not, why do you use us?)

5   Are you happy with our service? Do you have any complaints?

6   Are there any ways our service could be improved?

7   What are your buying plans at this moment? Do you plan to buy more, less, or the same as this time last year?

8   How have your needs altered? How do you think they will alter in the future?

9   How would you compare our competitors to us?

10   How much do you know about our company? What information about our company and products could be of help to you? (Or when can I come and see you?)

11   Thank you for taking part in this questionnaire – is there anything else you would like to add?

Often by conducting this exercise, your staff will find that sales improve. If not, you will now have the material to create the solution. Most customers will be impressed by the interest you are taking in them, and this in itself will help distinguish you from your competitors.

GAINING REFERRALS

Companies can be your best source of leads. They do not even need to have bought your products. At the end of every sales presentation (and after a sale has been made), your salespeople should be trained to ask something like: 'You've seen our product, Mr Jones, and how it can be of use to companies like yours. Are there any other companies in your field (or in your area/which you supply) who might benefit from them?' Always specify what sort of companies (for example 'in your field') to help focus the customer's attention. Feed them names, suggestions, until they give you something back. And don't just accept the name of the company – get its location and the name of someone you can talk to (probably the person your contact talks to).

Your staff then have a perfect introduction to that company: 'Hello, is that Mr Jones? I was just talking to Ms Stephens of the Widget Company and she suggested I gave you a call.'

As part of your daily figure-taking you can ask how many referrals each person has obtained, or you can include this section on your customer service records. If you don't remind salespeople and build it into the system they always forget – or are too scared to ask.

AFTER-SALES SERVICE

Too many salespeople fight shy of contacting customers again once they have made a sale. This is usually due to fear or guilt – guilt because the salesperson thinks he/she 'talked the customer into buying', and fear that the customer may have a complaint or may be angry. If your staff are trained how to sell properly and honestly, there should be no grounds for this.

However, you will still need to ensure that after-sales calls are performed regularly and effectively. Depending on your product/service, you will probably want to contact your customers one month and three months after purchase (a computer system can enforce this). Customers should be asked:

O   How are they and their business progressing?
O   How are they enjoying your product? What benefits are they deriving from it?

If customers show any hesitancy, the salesperson should remind them why they chose your product – and why it was the right decision. If they have any problems or complaints, it is better to help resolve them, than let them fester and so lose your customer (see 'Handling complaints' for more details).

The salesperson should then enquire about the customer's future buying plans (if relevant) and finally ask for referrals: can the customer think of anyone else who might benefit from your product? Or has anyone particularly admired their purchase?

HANDLING COMPLAINTS

Poorly handled complaints do not just lose you current customers, they can lose you future ones as well: research shows that customers will tell, on average, ten other people about complaints which they don't feel were handled well. You must establish with your staff set procedures for handling complaints. These may vary for different types of customers, but the following framework is fairly universal:

- Listen to customers' complaints in full. Thank them for bringing the matter to your attention and don't try to dismiss it out of hand.

- Write the complaint down, and repeat it back to the customer to make sure you have understood. Show concern. This removes much of the customer's frustration.

- Never say anything which might indicate that the customer has bought a bad product, or that your company is always receiving complaints.

- Do not act defensively. Do not take the complaint personally. Never argue with the customer.

- Do not instantly apologize – it may turn out that the customer is to blame, not your company – but do say that you are sorry that they have this problem. If your product is clearly covered by a warranty, you should set your customer's mind at rest immediately.

- Ask any questions which might clarify the situation.

- Ask your customers what, realistically, they would like the company to do. This is important. If you decide on a response without consulting your customer, you risk doing either too much or too little. Do not promise anything to your customer at this stage, unless such action is standard practice.

- Tell your customers what you will do next. Usually this will mean referring the matter to the sales manager and investigating the problem immediately. If there are standard procedures for complaint handling, explain these to the customer. Give a definite date/time by which you will report to them. Make sure the customer is satisfied with this, then keep to it come what may.

- Sometimes it helps to enable the customer to see things from your company's point of view (for example, 'I'm sure you'll appreciate that if we were obliged to do ... every time a customer had this problem, we wouldn't be able to offer this service at all.') However, this may sometimes worsen the situation. Always make the customer feel special, and show that you care.

- As soon as you have a solution, report back to your customer and make sure they are satisfied. If necessary, explain the reasons for this solution. Confirm the time for your next call or meeting.

- If the customer is not satisfied, investigate further.

- Keep full written details of all complaints and their outcome.

(Note: these guidelines are repeated in Course 12 of the companion volume to this book, *Training the Sales Team*.)

It must be a question of company policy how you respond to complaints, and what warranties and compensation you offer. However, wherever repeat business is at stake, these factors should really be determined by what the customer thinks is reasonable.

CONCLUSION: LOOKING TO THE FUTURE

Where does your future business lie? With your future customers. If you find yourself serving a declining or contracting market, you will have long-term problems which must be addressed now. Are there other parallel, but growing, markets which you could supply? This is really a marketing issue, but the problem can first be spotted on the sales floor.

Assuming that a contracting market is not a problem, how can you secure your future? Which of your customers are expanding? How can you better serve their needs? Companies must look at ways of ensuring that their products or services evolve over the years (hence computer manufacturers provide customers with upgrade paths which effectively lock out the competition). Service contracts can help guarantee future business and should be promoted even if they are effectively loss-leaders. What long-term services can you provide (possibly for free) which will encourage your customers to keep buying from you? For instance, some companies provide their customers with free marketing surveys, or free operational audits, or their service agreements will demand that all future equipment is fitted by their own engineers to ensure compatibility.

11

RECRUITING THE SALES TEAM – FINDING THE RIGHT PEOPLE

As a sales manager, your success or failure will ultimately depend on three factors:

○ The quality of your company and products.
○ The quality of your leadership.
○ The quality of your salespeople.

It follows that recruiting and developing the right people is necessary for the continued growth and success of your team. On the positive side, recruitment offers you one of the best means of significantly improving the attitude and calibre of your sales force. On the other hand, a poor recruitment decision can cost thousands of pounds in terms of wasted time, effort, and lost sales. This chapter and Chapter 12 will take you through the entire recruitment and selection process. It will suggest how to get the best out of recruitment, and will identify the pitfalls to avoid. This chapter covers the following subjects:

○ Staff turnover – good or bad?
○ Why do staff leave?
○ Identifying your requirements
○ The recruitment specification
○ Sourcing:

– Advertising
– Recruitment agencies
– Referrals
– School-leavers/university graduates.

STAFF TURNOVER – GOOD OR BAD?

Sometimes, of course, you will recruit new staff because of expansion or because members of your team have been promoted into different areas. In most cases, you will be recruiting to replace someone who has left your company – either voluntarily or through your prompting.

A high turnover of staff is not unusual in sales. It is quite normal for companies to have annual turnovers of 20 per cent or more, and there are companies in the service sector operating successfully with rates of 40 per cent and even 50 per cent! The reasons why staff leave vary from case to case, but there are two common themes: good performers leave to develop their careers and poor performers leave because they have not made enough sales.

Generally speaking, sales managers will try to retain the good performers and keep them motivated for as long as they can, and will want to identify and either improve or remove poor performers as soon as possible.

From this perspective, we can see that some staff turnover is beneficial to the sales team: it encourages new ideas; it establishes a healthy results-only atmosphere (where staff know there is no room for slackers); it promotes a feeling of change and dynamism. Also there are some people – the demotivated, the continual complainers, the shirkers – who every sales manager is delighted to see go.

If too many people join and leave your team, for whatever reason, the results can be damaging. These are some of the most common problems:

- Poor staff morale
- Loss of expertise
- Poor customer relations
- Lack of team spirit
- Lost sales
- Time and cost of training.

POOR STAFF MORALE

When people leave of their own free will (especially when they have been successful), there is often an implied criticism of your company or style of management. This can reinforce any discontent within your team, and can give the staff the feeling they are on a sinking ship. This in turn can inspire them to leave.

On the other hand, when salespeople leave at your bidding, staff can be demotivated if they think you have been unduly harsh or unreasonable. Never appear to single out individuals. Never gloat at their misfortune or seem insensitive to their feelings. When you dismiss, state your reasons clearly but tactfully. Avoid making other staff feel needlessly insecure.

LOSS OF EXPERTISE

Can you afford to lose experienced salespeople? Experienced, committed staff will not only generate consistent sales, but will share their sales skills and market knowledge with newer team-members. They will also contribute most to the team's 'character', morale and perseverance.

POOR CUSTOMER RELATIONS

Customers want stable relationships with their suppliers. They want to deal with the same person over a long period of time. A new recruit will not understand the customer's needs as well as your competitors, and may not have the personal 'prestige' to even get past the receptionist. If customers think you have a high staff turnover, they will take this as a reflection on the quality of your company.

LACK OF TEAM SPIRIT

Team spirit is necessary for successful management (see Chapter 4 for a full treatment of this topic). It cannot be generated overnight.

LOST SALES

Every day your team lacks a salesperson is a day when less sales are made. New salespeople are not immediately productive but require training and induction.

TIME AND COST OF TRAINING

Induction and training take up the time of your recruits (which you are paying for) and your own even more valuable and costly time. A detailed guide to training and inducting recruits will be found in *Training the Sales Team*, the companion volume to this book.

WHY DO STAFF LEAVE?

Whenever staff do leave, either voluntarily or through your prompting, review the situation:

○ Why did they leave?
○ What could be done to avoid this?

WHEN STAFF LEAVE OF THEIR OWN ACCORD

Reasons why staff leave might be purely negative:

○ Couldn't do the job
○ Boredom
○ Not appreciated by management
○ No job satisfaction
○ No opportunity to gain new skills
○ No opportunity to progress
○ Poor pay
○ Poor working conditions
○ Poor training
○ Poor company morale.

Or they may be because of better conditions *elsewhere*:

○ Better pay
○ Promotion
○ More interesting work
○ Better location
○ Opportunity to develop career.

You can do something about many of these factors yourself. If you do not want to lose talented staff, you should regularly review your pay, conditions, opportunities and so on to see how they might be improved. See Chapters 4, 5 and 7 for suggestions on improving motivation, job satisfaction and career progression in particular.

You must also recognize that staff do need to change jobs from time to time to develop their careers. In these instances, you can honestly congratulate them and turn their success into a selling point for your own company: by working with you, staff enhance their career opportunities.

WHEN STAFF LEAVE THROUGH THEIR FAILURE TO DO THE JOB

Before you recruit a replacement, review the reasons why the person failed. Common reasons for new recruits leaving are:

○ Poor training.
○ Not given clear tasks to achieve.
○ Not given quick, honest feedback about their performance.
○ Recruit felt excluded from the group or neglected by management.
○ Recruit allowed to adopt poor work patterns and standards.

- Recruit put under too much pressure.
- Recruit did not like the company.
- Recruit was not motivated to succeed.
- Recruit simply could not sell in this environment.

When more experienced staff leave, the reasons are more likely to be complex. The following answers are typical:

- Salesperson consistently failed to achieve sales targets.
- Salesperson lost interest in the job.
- Salesperson became more lax or ill-disciplined.
- Breakdown in communication/rapport between manager and salesperson.

When you recruit next, you will want to take these reasons into consideration and try to prevent them occurring again – either by recruiting a different sort of person or by treating your staff differently.

IDENTIFYING YOUR REQUIREMENTS

The next stage in the recruitment process is to decide what sort of person you want to recruit. This will be determined by the following considerations:

- What they will have to do.
- How soon you need them to produce sales.
- What potential they need for future development.
- The working environment.
- The salary you can afford.

This will in turn help you to determine what *skills, knowledge* and *personal qualities* the person must have. What do we mean by these three terms?

Skills and knowledge are the sales ability and market/product knowledge your recruits need to be able to do the job. Identify these from your staff's job description (see Chapter 4 for details) and from the criteria (the scale of values) you use to assess your staff (Chapter 8 covers this topic). Both skills and knowledge can be learnt, but the sooner you need your recruits to perform, the more they will need to know already.

Personal qualities, on the other hand, are what a salesperson is born with. They can be developed and encouraged, but they cannot be taught from scratch. Before we study the recruitment specification in detail, it is worth paying these personal qualities some attention.

Almost all research on recruiting sales staff lists the three most important factors in determining sales success as attitude, personality and aptitude. If you recruit someone who does not have the right personal qualities, your chances of turning him or her into a successful salesperson will be virtually nil. By aptitude we mean the ability to learn and apply sales skills. Attitude and personality vary from company to company and market to market. In deciding the right attitude and personality for your team, ask yourself the following:

- What qualities do my top performers have in common?
- What qualities do our customers look for?
- What sort of person will contribute to the sales team as a whole?

Research has identified the following ten qualities as the most common for sales success:

1   High personal goals and ambitions
2   Positive attitude (realistic but optimistic)

3   Warm, friendly personality (ability to get on with people easily)
4   Determination
5   Quick-wittedness
6   Excellent appearance and communication skills (high self-image)
7   Interest, enthusiasm and ability to convey them
8   Capacity for hard work
9   Capacity for self-improvement (always tries to do better)
10 Rehearsal, planning, organization.

There are other qualities to include: honesty, integrity, a sense of humour, and the motivation to earn and spend money. You will probably also want to recruit someone who will fit in with (and be part of) the team and someone who will feel at ease in whatever conditions, environments and situations come with the work.

The more of these qualities your recruits display, the greater their potential for success.

THE RECRUITMENT SPECIFICATION

Taking these considerations into account, draw up a complete recruitment specification. This will work as a blueprint for your entire recruitment process. It should include the following:

- Title
- Job description
- Personal qualities required
- Minimum skills required (and length of experience)
- Skills preferred
- Minimum knowledge required (what market or technical knowledge is necessary?)
- Knowledge preferred
- Suitable background (job, market and so on). Do your most successful salespeople share similar backgrounds?
- Salary on offer (What are on-target earnings including commission scheme? Will you guarantee commission for the first few months?)
- Benefits on offer
- Future prospects (Where will the person be in 1, 2 and 3 years' time? This will help determine the calibre of person you want).

Before you begin trying to find this person, ask yourself if your expectations are realistic. Common dangers to avoid are:

- Specification too narrow: restricts search to too few people, and screens out people who would be suitable.
- Specification too ideal: are all these criteria really necessary? Did all your successful staff meet them when they joined?
- Specification too broad: this effectively means you don't have a clear enough idea of who you want to recruit.
- Salary not right.

If there is an obvious conflict between the person you need to recruit and the salary you can offer, you must review the situation carefully before progressing. As a general rule, it is better to recruit someone who does not have all the experience but has the right personal qualities and potential, rather than recruit an experienced salesperson who is 'going cheap' but has little ability to grow. Successful salespeople never 'go cheap'.

SOURCING

Once you have decided on the person you want, you need to examine the sources available. These are:

- Advertising
- Recruitment agencies
- Referrals
- School-leavers/university graduates.

These sources are reviewed in the remaining sections of this chapter.

ADVERTISING

Advertising enables you to present your opportunity to prospective employees on your terms. In effect it 'sells' your job. Generally advertising will provide you with a large supply of candidates fairly quickly (within a few hours of publication for newspapers). There are various points to consider before placing your advertisement.

The right medium

Where will you reach the people you want to recruit? This is a complex issue which we can only examine briefly.

National newspapers are suitable for prestigious or national companies but they are relatively expensive and will not be read by people looking for local sales positions. Regional newspapers will produce strong local response, and are less expensive, but will you be addressing the right calibre of reader? The trouble with both national and regional papers is that they are read by the general public, and you may find yourself fending off numerous general enquiries.

As an alternative you may consider the range of specialist and trade magazines and journals, many of which carry recruitment advertising. You are more likely to find a computer sales consultant reading a computer trade weekly, for instance, than your local newspaper.

You must also make sure that the publication you are considering is an established recruitment medium. Some newspapers, for instance, have reputations for recruiting certain types of staff on certain days, and will be read by those people who are looking for work.

Finally, is the publication suitable for your company? Does it add glamour and prestige to your job or does it detract from it?

The size and style

Be guided by other companies' advertisements: yours should be equally large and well-designed for you to attract the same calibre of response. If you have doubts, refer to a professional advertising agency.

The cost

Advertising which works is rarely cheap, but advertising which doesn't is certainly not. When considering cost, you must accept the fact that you are paying for something which may not work. Be consoled that if it does work, advertising will probably be far more cost-effective than using a recruitment agency.

The wording

There is no one method which will guarantee response. The following are guidelines:

- Always include the name of your company, what your company does (in positive terms), the title, the location, the salary and benefits on offer (be fairly specific).
- Sell the job: what is the opportunity? Why should someone want to work for you?

Has this job arisen through expansion? What prospects are there? But be realistic or people won't take you seriously.
- State minimum requirements (and mention any particularly valuable skills).
- Give a personal contact name and phone number (day and evening).
- Make the job sound exciting and make the need to respond urgent!

Before writing your advertisement, read others in the paper you are planning to use: which would you respond to and why?

When it doesn't work

Don't keep backing a loser. Never accept the old advertising sales-line that you need to repeat an advertisement to make it work. If your advertisement does not attract the number or calibre of response you need, one of five factors can be wrong: the wording, the medium, the size, the style – or the job. Of these the two most likely to be wrong are the wording and the medium. Review both ruthlessly before deciding where next to advertise.

The response

First impressions count, and the way you handle initial response from an advertisement will affect the way candidates regard you. There is nothing worse than for applicants to ring up in their lunch break (the only time they can talk), to be told you are unavailable. Don't book meetings for days you are advertising. Eat your lunch at your desk.

The initial telephone 'interview'

When you handle response, always be warm and friendly. Start by asking the person for their name, and why they are interested in the advertisement. Remember that you have to judge from this conversation whether to interview this person or not. Likewise, they are going to be forming an impression of *you*.

First ask yourself 'How does this person sound on the phone?' Are they bright, enthusiastic? Are they asking you questions? Are they telling you why they are suitable for the job? Remember that a good salesperson should be doing all these things automatically.

Then concentrate on the person's background. How many years experience do they have? Doing what? What are they doing at the moment? Is it relevant to what you want? Why are they looking to leave? What do they want to do next? Then turn this around: what do they want to know about your opportunity?

Now decide if you are interested, and ask them if they are. Have you sold yourself and your opportunity well enough? Is there anything else you need to mention? Or are there aspects of the job you should warn the person about (for example, it involves a lot of travelling)?

If all has gone well, arrange an interview. There is a limit to how much you can tell about a person over the phone (and vice versa) and if you talk for too long you can oversell the position. Arrange interviews as soon as possible. Do not wait for a c.v. – tell them to bring one with them.

If you are unsure, you can delay your decision by asking them to send in a c.v. with a covering letter outlining why they think they are suitable. Tell them you ask all potential candidates to do this.

Alternatively you could confront the person with your reservation and see how they respond: 'My one reservation is that you have no experience of face-to-face sales – is there any reason why I ought to overlook this?' If they cannot overcome this sort of objection they will never succeed as a salesperson!

RECRUITMENT AGENCIES

If you try to recruit by advertising, you are faced with many problems, as we have seen: the time to organize, plan and devise the advertisement; spending the money 'up front';

handling and screening the response. Recruitment agencies will remove these problems by providing you with a shortlist of suitable, pre-screened candidates. Furthermore, their service is free until you actually recruit someone. Even then they may offer money-back guarantees covering the applicant's induction period. Recruitment agencies are not cheap, and you must be prepared to pay from 15 to 20 per cent of your recruit's starting salary (usually including OTE) once a placement has been made.

If you have the budget for it, it is worth trying recruitment agencies (providing they operate a 'no placement, no fee' policy) as they can usually offer you a choice of suitably qualified and experienced applicants at very short notice. If nothing else, this will give you an idea of what is available, and you can ask the consultancies' advice on such matters as starting salary and market conditions. Some consultants also offer an advertising service which, while more expensive than advertising direct, may also be more effective. Ask and compare prices, and don't be afraid to negotiate. Most agencies will offer discounts in exchange for 'sole agency status' (dealing with them alone for a limited period) or for prompt payment.

A professional recruitment consultant should start by taking a full recruitment specification from you (if they do not, find someone who does). They may offer advice on the attractiveness of the position and the sort of person you are likely to get. They may already have people registered with them who are suitable. If they have, allow them to sell their applicants to you over the telephone, and be prepared to interview them straight away, subject to their c.v.'s being faxed across – if you are not able to move this quickly, your competitors will.

When interviewing applicants sent by agencies, always ask the applicant what they have been told about your opportunity. A good agency will have already sold its applicant on the job, which makes your life easier, but a bad one might have exaggerated (or omitted) some aspects.

If you wish to make an offer to an agency applicant, always do so via the agency. This is because recruitment consultants are trained to present offers to applicants professionally, and will handle objections and queries. They may also be aware of other offers your applicant is considering and can advise you on how best to proceed.

REFERRALS

Your staff may already know people who would be ideal for your position. Always let your own staff know you are recruiting (if this is tactful), and the sort of person you are looking for. Some companies so favour this method of recruitment that they pay bounties to staff or offer free meals and other incentives. Certainly it has advantages: staff will not recommend people who will reflect badly on them or who they know to have poor records, attitudes and so on; also the whole process encourages them to think positively about your organization. There are some disadvantages: do you want to recruit personal friends of other members of staff – could this lead to tensions within the team? What if you think the person referred is unsuitable – could this be embarrassing for all concerned?

SCHOOL-LEAVERS/UNIVERSITY GRADUATES

If you regularly need new trainees, you could investigate the possibility of recruitment from schools and universities. These bodies generally have careers advisers who will be happy to organize tie-ins and offer advice. Graduates and school-leavers may take longer to train, but they are cheaper to recruit and can provide you with fresh blood. They can also be trained in exactly the way you wish, with no bad habits or attitudes. There is also the chance you may recruit someone with real star potential, who within six months of joining could be one of your top performers. These high fliers are obviously much harder to attract later in their careers.

There are drawbacks with recruiting raw trainees. As they have no track record, it is harder to judge whether an applicant has real potential. Likewise, school-leavers and graduates may not really know what they want to do – they might find working 40 hours a week harder than they expected – and may abruptly change their mind and leave. They may also be naive about business practices and handle situations with less maturity than more experienced staff.

SUMMARY

In this chapter we have reviewed how to draw up a recruitment specification and investigate the sources of suitable applicants. In Chapter 12 we examine the most effective means of interviewing and assessing these applicants.

12

RECRUITING THE SALES TEAM – INTERVIEWING AND OFFERING

Interviews are complex processes. In interviewing, your first aims will be to establish the right relationship with the person and to assess their suitability in terms of their skills, knowledge and personality. You will also be trying to sell yourself and your company to them, making them want to work for you, while giving them a full and accurate description of what the job actually entails. You will have to answer your applicant's questions and perhaps reassure them or persuade them that your opportunity is better than others they are considering. You will also be trying to read between the lines of their answers to gauge their true feelings and true level of interest.

This chapter explains how to interview and assess your applicants effectively, as well as pointing out some of the problems to avoid. It is divided into the following sections:

- Planning the interview process
- The application form
- How to interview
- Questions to ask
- Information to prepare
- Reviewing your interviews
- The second interview
- Taking up references
- Tests
- Making offers
- Making rejections
- Conclusion.

PLANNING THE INTERVIEW PROCESS

Always plan to interview your applicants at least twice. Use the first interview to assess candidates' experience and outlook, to present information about the company and job, and to screen out people who are unsuitable or uninterested. Use the second interview to get to know the candidate in more depth and resolve any queries either of you might have. If you try to combine all this in one interview, you will either make mistakes or rush your candidates. This may cause them to reject your offer or regret accepting it later.

Decide in advance the main questions you will ask candidates and make sure you ask each one the same questions. This is the only way of comparing like with like. Do allow yourself the scope to let the interview develop naturally. Structured interviews are good, but they give you less opportunity to assess the other person's character.

Give yourself enough time – 1 hour for a first interview, 2 hours for a second interview – but curtail the interview if there is obviously no point in continuing.

Always ask applicants to bring copies of their c.v. with them. This gives you a talking-point and allows you to assess their ability to present themselves attractively on paper.

If you are involving other staff in the interview process (maybe team leaders or senior salespeople), give them time to prepare questions and allow them to review the candidate's career beforehand.

Remember that poor interviewing reflects badly on your company. Anyone who has not interviewed staff before should be given training. You should also review the condition of the room you will use for interviewing – what does it say about your organization?

THE APPLICATION FORM

When applicants arrive for interview, they are often given application forms to fill in. There are many pros and cons to this. The advantages are:

- Application forms give you the information you want in the order you want it.
- Application forms help you compare different candidates easily.
- A prestigious application form can prepare the candidate for interview.
- Application forms require candidates to present their thoughts clearly and legibly in written form.

Application forms are most useful when candidates have not provided their own c.v.'s. The disadvantages of using them are:

- They waste time at the start of the interview.
- The forms can appear bureaucratic.
- Application forms generally ask candidates to copy out information which is better presented on their own c.v.'s.
- If you have specific questions you want to ask all candidates, it is better to ask them during the interview.

For the reasons above, it is best not to use application forms unless absolutely necessary. If you wish to use them, keep the amount of factual data to a minimum, and concentrate instead on information which most c.v.'s will not give you. The following are good questions to ask:

- What would you list as your three main strengths?
- What would you give as your three main weaknesses?
- Why have you applied for this position?
- How would you define the sales process?
- As a salesperson, what are your main aims?
- What attracts you to sales as a career?
- Describe in not more than 50 words your ideal holiday.

Make sure your application forms are designed with the same care and attention as your sales documents. Make sure also that they are in keeping with any relevant legislation or guidelines concerning discrimination on grounds of sex or race.

HOW TO INTERVIEW

The following are guidelines:

- Plan your interview and the questions you are going to ask beforehand. If you already have information on your candidate, read it in advance and note any apparent discrepancies or points of interest that you will wish to discuss.
- Enter the interview with an open mind.
- The first 20 seconds of the interview are critical, as both you and the interviewee will be receiving and giving first impressions. Offer the person your hand, be welcoming, smile, put them at their ease. First impressions can prejudice the entire interview (either favourably or unfavourably). As first impressions play a vital part in sales, they do have some bearing on the candidate's suitability. Minimize the risk of their clouding your judgement by writing them down on your interview notes, and then making a conscious effort not to judge the person in those terms.
- As the interview unfolds, write down all of your applicant's important answers, plus your observations of their behaviour, attitude and so on. Don't rely on your memory.
- Establish good eye-contact where natural. Note the person's body language: are they relaxed and outgoing or nervous and reticent?
- Avoid dominating the conversation. Ask your applicants open questions that enable them to elaborate on answers. Encourage them to express themselves in their own words, and to ask questions. Often the questions applicants ask reveal what their true thoughts and concerns are.
- Show interest in (and respect for) your applicant's career and achievements to date.
- Give an accurate and realistic job description which will prepare the applicant for the job. Tell applicants exactly what you will expect in terms of sales figures, attitude and hours worked. If this frightens them, it's better to know now.
- Sell the benefits of your sales team: in-depth ongoing training, career opportunities, fair results-orientated commission scheme, dynamic flexible working environment, excellent sales support staff, clear goal-setting, regular reviews, weekly sales meetings, as well as superb market-leading products. How many more can you think of?
- Always ask your applicants if they are interested – and why.
- Tell the applicant what happens next. If you are interested in taking things further, by all means say so, but let them know you are seeing others as well.
- Make sure that you conduct the interview in the spirit of equal opportunities and in accordance with legislation concerning sexual or racial discrimination. It is important that you judge (and are seen to judge) each applicant solely in terms of their ability to do the job.
- Close the interview by thanking the applicant for their time.

QUESTIONS TO ASK

During the interview ask open-ended questions which encourage your candidate to talk freely. The four most effective questions you can ask are:

- What do you most enjoy about your present position?
- What would you like to see improved?
- Why are you here on interview?
- Where do you see yourself in three years' time?

The first question is particularly effective in revealing the candidate's true nature – it usually catches people off-guard. Always be suspicious of someone who can find nothing enjoyable in their present position – will they find anything in yours? Other good questions are:

- What are your main achievements to date – and why?
- What are your main strengths?
- What are your main weaknesses?
- What do you think you could bring to our team?
- How would you try to provide our customers with better service?
- Why should I offer you this position?

Always question your applicants about their current position:

- Describe one problem you had in your present job. How have you overcome it?
- Why did you join your present company?
- Why do you want to leave?
- Why do you think we could offer you a better career than your present company?
- How would you describe your present work?

For any question to be effective, you must ask it sincerely and naturally, not as if you have just read it out of a book, and you must be genuinely interested in your applicants' answers – are they telling the truth? When applicants describe experiences, show interest and use questions to probe further: 'How did you find that?' 'What were your reactions to that?' 'How would you compare…?'

INFORMATION TO PREPARE

As well as a full job description, prepare information on your commission structure and company benefits, together with a selection of your corporate literature. The following are some of the questions which applicants typically ask interviewers (and which you should be prepared to answer):

- What level would I be joining at?
- What is the starting salary? When is it reviewed?
- What sort of training do you offer?
- What are my opportunities in the company – and how soon?
- What are the main benefits of working for your company?
- What are you looking for in your candidates?
- Do you think I am suitable for the position?

REVIEWING YOUR INTERVIEWS

Review each candidate immediately after the interview, even if you have other people to see: your memory will fade within even an hour of the meeting. Points to review are:

❖ What is my overall impression of the person? Can I justify it with reference to specifics?

❖ Could they do the job?

❖ Could I work with them, and would they fit into the team?

❖ Did they seem motivated, enthusiastic and committed?

❖ Did they make an effort to communicate with me?

❖ How good were their communication skills?

❖ How smart was their appearance?

❖ Did they have a good understanding of the selling process?

- Did they ask lots of relevant questions?
- Did they seem able to handle my objections and queries?
- Were they ever tongue-tied or at a loss for an answer?
- Do they have a strong, mature character?
- Will they be able to cope with the volume and type of sales work we have here?
- What are my main concerns about this person?
- Did they make any undue criticisms of their current or former employers?
- Did they blame others for their own failings instead of facing up to them?
- If I offer them, will they accept for the right reasons? And will they stay?

Below are some of the common reasons (sensible reasons, that is) why applicants fail interviews. If your applicants' behaviour is described in the list, you are probably right to fail them:

- Poor appearance
- Overbearing, aggressive or conceited attitude
- Poor voice, diction, grammar
- No interest or enthusiasm
- Nervousness, no poise
- Overemphasis on money
- Impatience, wants too much too soon
- Tactless
- Rude, discourteous
- No social understanding
- Failure to see things from a corporate standpoint
- Evasiveness
- Failure to ask questions about the job
- No consideration for others
- Intolerant or prejudicial attitudes
- Laziness
- Cynicism and sarcasm
- No sense of humour
- No appreciation of the value of experience or training
- Thinking he/she has all the answers
- Unwilling to accept criticism
- Inability to listen
- No respect for authority
- Unaccountable gaps in career
- Too many jobs
- Too many 'bad luck stories'
- Overfamiliarity
- Overformality.

THE SECOND INTERVIEW

The second interview should give your applicants the chance to ask you more about the company, to meet (or be interviewed by) some of your staff, and to have a better look around your site.

You will be seeking to establish your candidate's real interest in the position, and will want to clarify any points or queries which have been suggested by your review of their first interview. It is usually a good policy to express your concerns honestly and see how the person responds. At this stage you are not trying to sell the job so much as see if the person really is suitable – and keen.

If the candidate is being interviewed by other members of staff, make sure they are properly introduced and allow them plenty of time alone together (agree this in advance with your staff). Make sure that your staff are properly trained to interview, that they have prepared questions in advance and know how to 'sell' your company. If you have particular concerns about the applicant, you can ask your staff to investigate these. Review the interview with your staff as soon afterwards as possible.

If you think the candidate might be suitable, ask: 'If I offered you this position, would you take it?' You need to know what they really think about the position and what salary they would expect. Do they have any reservations? Or are they attending other interviews? If so, how does your opportunity compare?

Finally, let the person know when you will make your decision and ask whether this fits in with their plans.

After the second interview, compare your notes with those from your first interview. Do you now know them better? Has the interview resolved your initial concerns or raised new ones? Have any inconsistencies emerged? Did they get on well with your staff? Do you feel you can trust and believe in this person? Do you think they can – and will – do the job?

TAKING UP REFERENCES

Always check references. At the very least they protect you from employing people who have fabricated their entire careers (I've met more than one in sales). At best, a reference can confirm your own feelings and even resolve any lingering doubts. Do bear in mind that not all references are reliable: some managers take a perverse pleasure in denigrating previous employees; others irresponsibly praise people. Use your judgement. Also remember that legal considerations might restrict the detail of the reference. It is best to take all references orally first, over the phone, as this enables you to ask informal questions and 'read between the lines'. You can then ask for confirmation in writing if need be. Good questions to ask are:

- Why, in your opinion, did the person leave your company?
- Would you employ this person again?
- What do you think his/her main strengths and contributions were?
- As a manager, what were the main problems you had with him/her?
- I am thinking about offering this person a job, but my one concern is xxx – what are your thoughts on this?

Never take up a reference from someone's current employer without the candidate's express permission.

TESTS

Testing is becoming increasingly popular. In a sales context, the most relevant form is psychometric testing to determine the person's personal qualities (attitude, aptitude, personality). If your induction programme is expensive and time-consuming, or you find that the drop-out rate of recruits is unacceptable, you should seriously investigate testing for all second-interview candidates.

Of course, testing will only work if you know what you are looking for in advance. Done properly, psychometric testing should start with a full assessment of your recruitment specification, a profiling of the personal qualities of your ideal candidate, and how you assess staff in the job, so be prepared and remember that if you specify the wrong qualities, you will end up with the wrong results. Only ever use testing as a tool: never employ someone simply on the strength of a good test.

MAKING OFFERS

Putting an offer to someone is like selling them a product or a service. By the end of the second interview, you should have established whether the person is interested, what their concerns are, and – at least roughly – what sort of salary they would accept. You should also have arranged a time for you to contact them (or vice versa): this raises expectations nicely.

When you speak to the person, start by asking if they are still interested and whether they have any questions. If they did have concerns, you might mention these yourself, especially if you have solutions or suggestions to make. Provided everything looks positive, *then* make the offer. (There is nothing more ineffectual than offering someone a job if they are not sure they want it.)

Tell them everyone who met them was impressed/was excited/liked them, and that you personally are very pleased to offer them the job as you think they will do well. Pause to let the applicant register his or her excitement. Then give them the details of the starting position in the order of title, base salary, any guarantees, any benefits, first review, commission scheme.

Say that you will put everything in writing, then ask them for their initial reaction, and – if they are pleased – congratulate them straight away. Confirm that this means they will be accepting your offer, and ask if they are able to suggest a start-date and so on. Don't try to rush or pressurize someone at this stage – it can destroy the whole offer. If they request time to think it over and see it in writing, respect this, and ask when they can give you a decision – in most instances you should expect a firm answer within 24 hours of receiving the letter (or immediately after the next weekend). You should also ask if there is anything they are not sure about, and if they are waiting to hear from any other companies – if so, how does your opportunity compare?

MAKING REJECTIONS

As soon as you have decided not to proceed with an application, notify the person immediately. This is not just a question of courtesy but can affect your company's reputation in the recruitment market – all applicants hate finding out they were unsuccessful only by guesswork or hearsay. Bear in mind that people who are not right for you now might be in a few years' time or might know people who are. Applicants should be notified by letter. In the letter, always include the following:

- Thank them for attending the interview.
- Say you enjoyed meeting them and discussing their careers.
- Say that unfortunately on this occasion you do not wish to proceed with their application.
- Wish them every success in their careers.
- Welcome them to apply in the future (if they have potential).

Never give specific reasons why someone was unsuccessful. If pressed, the answer least likely to cause problems is 'the sheer number of suitably qualified applicants'.

You should keep records of all applicants you interview for positions. This means that if they apply in the future, you can gauge whether it is worth reconsidering them, and if you are ever accused of discrimination in the selection progress, you have the evidence to defend yourself.

CONCLUSION

As these two chapters show, selecting and recruiting the right staff is a complex and demanding task. It is also critical to the future success of your sales team. Always make recruitment a priority task and give it the time and consideration it deserves. Review your processes and selection criteria in the light of each recruit who either succeeds or fails.

13

TROUBLESHOOTING

Although we have reviewed a number of management problems throughout this book, there are certain challenges and difficulties you may encounter that deserve special attention. This chapter and Chapter 14 are intended to be a practical source of ideas and strategies for dealing with problems as and when they occur. I have tried to cover as wide a range of problems and solutions as possible. Use these chapters as a notebook or a think-tank, or for brainstorming sessions. Problems we deal with in this chapter are as follows:

- Lack of motivation and poor morale
- Falling sales
- Only one or two high performers in the team
- Staff not working long/hard enough
- Staff not doing their work thoroughly
- High staff turnover.

In Chapter 14, we then examine problems related to staff's behaviour:

- Managing difficult staff
- Unruly behaviour and how to discipline staff.

First, let's start by reviewing a few general principles about troubleshooting and problem-solving:

- Always look for the reason why: what you think is a problem may just be the symptom of the real problem.
- The only way to tackle a problem is enthusiastically and confidently: your solution may not be the right one but it may still work if you apply it with conviction.
- Never be afraid of admitting you've made a mistake.
- Wherever sensible, try to involve your staff in the problem and its solution. Often they will see things from different perspectives.

LACK OF MOTIVATION AND POOR MORALE

Can you distinguish between a lack of motivation (no one motivated to work hard) and poor morale (low belief in team, the company or the service)? Which is affecting your staff? And is it affecting the whole team – or just certain individuals?

First of all, can you identify the reason for this? Is it a new problem? And what are its causes – the company or the market or the salespeople themselves? Typical reasons for lack of motivation include:

- Poor sales figures
- Some sort of change in working pattern/commission structure/company organization
- Boredom
- Exhaustion or tiredness
- Oppressive or faulty management
- Poor product or service
- Poor training
- Poor working conditions
- The time of the year – just after a bank holiday, for instance, or during particularly hot weather, can be bad times for morale.

If you can identify the problem, what can you do about it? Here are a range of options:

- Lift people out of a negative rut by reorganizing the office. Move chairs, desks, filing cabinets – anything! Many companies deliberately re-seat staff every three months. Staff often dislike this, but the movement 'wakes people up', breaks up cliques, and creates the impression that 'something is happening'.
- Can you launch a competition? If your staff's grounds for dissatisfaction are genuine and serious, a competition may seem trivial and irrelevant, but in other circumstances it may be just the thing, especially if it offers a deliberately 'fun' prize, like a day out at a theme park. Better still, if the whole team is feeling jaded, why not hire a bus and take everyone to a theme park the next weekend?
- If you have senior sales staff, this is where you should be consulting with them, asking for their opinion on the problem and its solution. Give them each a particular motivational task (for example, ask one to lead the cold calling, another to come in early).
- Often demotivation stems from poor administrative or office support – is there anything you could do to improve things – or just change them?
- At the next sales meeting, confront the issue head-on: what's wrong? What can we do to make things better? Why is everyone so miserable? Just by listening to problems you can improve the atmosphere.
- Are certain management practices causing these problems? In which case how can we modify them or explain to the staff why we need them?
- If you don't have a good training programme, or have let it lapse, now's the best time to restart it. Training helps people view their jobs in a new, professional light. It can encourage them to take more pride in their skills and abilities. It can build teamwork. Try something new, like a group role-play session, or hire a video camera and film consultants in role-play situations. For further ideas see the companion volume to this book, *Training the Sales Team*.
- A particularly good training session to improve morale is one based on 'What are our Unique Selling Points – in what ways are we better than our competitors?' Each person on the team has to contribute one idea to the list. Then ideas are swapped and the next day each person has to offer three sales-lines incorporating that USP. Then each person has to think of one way in which competitors' products appear to be better. Once again, ideas are swapped (by the sales manager) and the next day each salesperson has to produce three responses to the competitors' apparent advantages. Award prizes such as bottles of wine for the best answers.
- Try a pep talk. For the pep talk to work, it must be impeccably prepared and you must deliver it with absolute conviction. Acknowledge the problems the staff are

facing, then tell them why they can't just lie down and die. The solution to most motivation problems is just hard work, plus a few new ideas, even if all you are doing is reinventing the wheel. Tell them what they're going to be doing – working harder, and working smarter – and that if they trust you and do what you tell them, they will succeed. The message of trust, team spirit and hard work, backed up by an implied threat if necessary, is the essence of the successful pep talk. It also helps if you can get the staff thinking for themselves: what else can they try to improve their performance? What are the most common problems they're all facing? Any ideas?

○ Can you work alongside the sales force? Can you move your office into the sales floor, or accompany them on client visits, or make canvassing calls with them? If staff see you doing their work, having the same problems as they have, and overcoming them, they will gain in confidence.

○ Can you trace the problems to an individual or clique of malcontents? If you can, your only solution is to confront them. Sometimes poor morale is caused by one popular, but bored or incompetent salesperson: if all else fails it is probably best to get rid of him/her as quickly as possible. Set the troublemaker a punishing set of targets. Put him to work by himself. Or, if you want to keep him, put him in charge of organizing company parties or nights out (but nothing more important than this). Make him worry about people blaming him if they don't enjoy themselves!

FALLING SALES

Probably your worse problem – after all, your main responsibility as sales manager is ensuring that group or company sales targets are met.

The first thing to do is to identify why sales are falling. Typical reasons may be:

○ Poor morale, motivation
○ Low expectations
○ Competition from other companies' products
○ Recession
○ Poor training
○ Poor service
○ Too few sales executives (or too few good ones)
○ Inefficient work practices.

Very often poor sales figures are due to poor morale and lack of enthusiasm, resulting in less work being done, with less flair and less interest. Under these circumstances staff will usually blame everything – market, company products, sales management, time of year – except themselves. This is where a pep talk is most useful (see previous section for how to go about this).

Another of the most common reasons for poor sales is that staff get used to underperforming, or think they cannot do any better. If this is the case, you must find a way of breaking the vicious circle. Start by telling them in no uncertain terms that the problem is simply their own lack of self-belief! If they trust your opinion (or have a healthy respect for your displeasure), this will start to solve the problem. Or do the job yourself, and show them how much more can be achieved. Make your staff increase the volume of their work by setting them strict targets for the number of phone-calls and visits: for example, increase these by 10 per cent a day until you've got the level you need. Doing this *by the day* is more immediate than doing it by the week.

When your sales are falling, time is of the essence. Here are some ideas for boosting sales revenue quickly:

- Identify the one basic task on which all sales depend. For most sales teams, this is the canvassing call. What can you do to improve or increase this? One company found their sales plummeting by 40 per cent in the first six months of the recent recession. They reacted by increasing the number of canvassing calls each consultant had to make from 20 to 50 a day. They also introduced strict monitoring of telephone calls to ensure they were done. The scheme met with some initial hostility but resulted in significantly improving canvassing returns. The increased workload, by keeping people busier, also improved morale. Staff morale rose again when they realized they weren't going to lose their jobs – and might actually make more sales. Alternatively, could you hire extra canvassing staff, paid on a semi-commission basis?
- Or maybe you have not a volume but a *quality* problem? Your staff are making enough calls, but they are not closing enough deals. Is this a marketing problem – should your products/services be improved, repositioned or repriced – or is this because of poor sales skills? Perhaps you, as sales manager, should take over closing the more difficult deals? Organize an intensive training course in closing and objection-handling – outside office hours. Are there any new objections which need to be addressed? Or is the problem that too many of your leads have not been qualified? Perhaps your staff are wasting their time with people who simply do not, or cannot, buy. If this is the case, you need to improve the volume of leads and introduce more rigorous qualifying procedures at the start of the sales process. (For details on how to do this, see Course 3 in the companion volume to this book, *Training the Sales Team*.)
- Have a one-to-one meeting with each salesperson in turn. As well as finding out what they think is happening, you must give each one precise goals aimed at breaking out of their sales ruts. By letting each person know you are relying on them and believe in them, you will help them to work harder.
- Maybe you can tighten up on discipline: are staff taking too many coffee-breaks? Are they unconcerned about their performance figures? Do they not take the job seriously? Be tough by all means, but never panic, or be cruel! Your team need you to be calm, determined, reliable – and confident of succeeding.
- Change your daily working structure (see Chapter 4 for ideas), placing more emphasis on customer contact, or direct phonework.
- Are you losing business to your competitors or are your customers simply buying less? The best way of investigating this is through a customer service questionnaire. (For an example and full discussion, see Chapter 10.)
- If sales are down because of market conditions, are your commission and sales targets still realistic? Remember the Expectancy theory of motivation (see in the Appendix to Chapter 3): if your staff no longer think their goals are achievable they will become demotivated. Can you introduce a different commission scheme without committing yourself to greater expenditure?
- Are there any other products or services which your customers also buy that you could sell? The solution might lie in expanding the range of add-on services you offer, or becoming agents for a complementary range of products.
- Can you re-focus your sales efforts? In most companies the majority of sales comes from a small, easily identifiable group of key clients, and most business is repeat business. How can you achieve more repeat business? Ask your staff to canvass through old order books, or visit all of their key accounts, or ring their key accounts once a week if this helps them discover new requirements more quickly. Employ the questionnaire method on key accounts as a matter of course. Is there any way you can establish further commitment to buy your goods or services? In a recession many companies are offering sole supplier agreements, including cheaper unit

costs and more flexible services in exchange for the customer agreeing not to buy from a competitor.
- Alternatively, you may decide that your key accounts are as fully developed as possible, and what you need is new customers. This is the perennial challenge of sales. How can you do it better? Explain the problem to the sales force. Ask them for ideas. Stage a competition for the greatest number of appointments with new clients in the next month. Can you provide them with a fresh source of new leads? Or is there a promotional offer which may help you break new accounts? Can you direct the entire effort of the sales force to canvassing for new business for a week? Or can you have everyone canvass for new business each day until they produce, say, three new leads?
- Can you *increase* the price of your goods? In a recession the first reaction may be to reduce prices. This is not always productive. In some markets, customers may only be buying when they have to, and will not buy more of your goods if they are cheaper. But if they *have to buy* your goods (or it is far more convenient for them to do so), you may even be able to raise prices (and hence sales revenue). This is true for companies selling goods or services on a commission basis (for example, broking, estate agency, recruitment and so on) – as the market has become more difficult, those companies who can still get results have often been able to charge more for their service.
- Where price does make a difference, be prepared to offer discounts. Are there ways you can use discounts to your advantage, to encourage repeat business or larger orders?
- Can you change your own work patterns to spend more time sitting next to salespeople, offering them advice, analysing their sales pitches, and so on?
- Is there anything more you can do to create a sales 'buzz'? If your staff sell by telephone, get them to make their calls standing up and don't let them put down their phones between calls. They may feel awkward to start with, but their phonework will be more dynamic. If your staff are in the field, how can you make them more positive? Ask them to ring into the office after every visit to tell you results and talk through the sales conversation: this will make them more aware of missed opportunities.
- Review your company's advertising and promotional strategy. Would you benefit from an improved logo, packaging and so on? How good is your company brochure? What does it say about you? After all the sales presentations have been made, buying decisions are often based on the company brochure. If yours is poorly worded or badly printed, you will lose out. Are there any additional promotional aids or visual displays you could give your staff? Do you need to review your advertising strategy? Sometimes advertising needs to be increased – or totally cut, and the money saved or invested in other forms of promotion, such as direct mail, or telephone canvassing.

ONLY ONE OR TWO HIGH PERFORMERS IN THE TEAM

A lack of high performers is a common phenomenon in most sales teams, and is only to be expected. A recent survey shows that the top 20 per cent of a sales force is likely to produce 40 per cent of sales, the next 60 per cent will produce 50 per cent, and the bottom 20 per cent no more than 10 per cent. Often, in fact, the dynamics of the team will only allow there to be one or two high performers at the same time. Sometimes 'irreplaceable' top performers leave, only to be almost immediately replaced by staff who had been only average before: what spurs people on is a sense that 'now their time has come' or that success is now achievable.

There is room for worry when you and your company are dependent on one or two high performers for most of your revenue. In some sales teams the top 30 per cent can produce as much as 70 per cent or even 80 per cent of the results – with potentially destabilizing consequences. If these salespeople leave, or stop producing, you could be in trouble – and usually they know it. Some high performers have been known to so dominate sales teams that they could expand their sales territories at will, and took over any trainee's business if it seemed profitable. This is management at its weakest and worst.

If you are afraid of getting into this predicament, the first thing, as always, is to analyse your current situation:

- Why are your top performers doing so well? Ability? Training? Or do they have the best territories? Never resent ability – be grateful for it. But if a salesperson is doing well because of a larger or more profitable territory, you need to be sure they are exploiting it fully. If they are, you have less to worry about (apart from other people's jealousy) – if they were to leave, you could replace them or divide the territory. If they are not, you should make changes.
- Why are the rest of your staff not doing better? Often the answer lies in inexperience, motivation or training. All of these you can rectify (see below).
- Is there any one thing to which the top performers would attribute their success, such as more canvassing, better closing techniques, more rapport with their customers, better product knowledge, longer hours, better phone technique, listening to their customers? Can you organize an intensive training course on this – perhaps even run by a top performer? Or if it is something easily quantifiable, like the number of canvass calls, or the number of new leads, organize a competition.
- Perhaps junior staff are losing orders through inexperience. You can probably improve here by personally taking over bids at the closing stages, or by working alongside the trainees as soon as things look hopeful. As long as you are not condescending and trainees still earn commission on sales you close for them, you will not offend or upset them.
- Perhaps most of the staff are demotivated, and it is only the self-motivated who are making sales. For ideas on how to handle this, see the section earlier in this chapter.

Finally, never let yourself be held to ransom by your high performers. Show them respect, yes, and do your best to keep them happy and give them scope to earn more. But never at the expense of other members of staff or the good interests of your company.

STAFF NOT WORKING LONG/HARD ENOUGH

Sometimes sales managers can be tempted to view all of their staff as lazy, incompetent, or both. Sometimes they are right. Quite often, they are committing one of the easiest mistakes in management. No one likes working for managers who regard their staff in this way – usually it is a sign of being out of touch, or of having no respect for the people they manage. And if staff *are* lazy or incompetent, managers should remember they were not born that way. Often the answer lies in the way they have been managed. But there are many times when management is not at fault and the blame lies fairly and squarely with the staff. We will examine these problems later in this section. But first, let's review those instances when management is at least partially to blame.

MANAGEMENT PARTIALLY TO BLAME

Typical reasons are:

1　　　The manager does not appear to work hard, or does not stay late.
2　　　The manager seems to avoid tasks he/she expects others to do.
3　　　Poor morale or motivation.
4　　　No team leadership.
5　　　Poor training programme.
6　　　Hard work is not adequately rewarded (either through commission or praise).
7　　　Staff are fed up with their manager ordering them to do things.

The manager does not appear to work hard, or does not stay late

The answer to this is obvious: if you are expecting staff to work to 6.30 or 7.00 every night (which in many offices is usually the best way to process paperwork and so on), then you should do the same. Set yourself tasks that keep you in the middle of the office, where you can see who is working late and can praise them the next day in front of everyone else. After two weeks or so, you will probably find that people start working longer hours of their own accord.

The manager seems to avoid tasks he/she expects others to do

An easy mistake to make, simply by being too busy. Of course you are not paid to do your salespeople's jobs for them (that's what they're there for!), but you should never be too busy to do each task with them every now and then, especially if it is a new, difficult or unpopular task, such as cold calling. Nothing else will more inspire your staff to work hard than if they see you setting the pace every morning.

Poor morale or motivation

For a full treatment of this topic, refer back to the section earlier in this chapter.

No team leadership

If people are not given goals and the means, encouragement and inspiration to achieve these goals, they will not work at their best. Refer to Chapters 1, 4 and 5 for more details on this problem and how to handle it.

Poor training programme

Does your training encourage hard work and motivation as the keys to sales success? Does it give your staff the skills to perform competently? If it does not, rectify this immediately with a 'refresher' programme.

Hard work is not adequately rewarded (either through commission or praise)

Does your commission put a ceiling on your staff's potential earnings? Do you significantly reward high achievers? Even more importantly, do you show respect and appreciation for those people who work above and beyond the strict terms of their contract? There is nothing more irritating than a boss with no gratitude – especially when he/she may have left hours earlier!

Staff are fed up with their manager ordering them to do things

Following on from the previous point: you cannot expect people to work longer or harder than they have to, unless they see the benefit, or need, of it. They will certainly resent being told to do so by their manager. Instead, as we have shown, set an example, or *sell* them the idea in terms of how it will benefit them. If your people have to work late, ask them; don't tell them. Or let them draw their own conclusions: how else do they propose to get their work done?

WHEN STAFF ARE IN THE WRONG

All of the suggestions above suppose that the manager is at least partially to blame for not getting his/her staff to work later or harder. There are many times when the staff, or certain members of the staff, *are* in the wrong: they are either not dedicating themselves to the task in hand or they are working poorly and ineffectively.

In these situations, you need to apply some measure of authority, not sweet words and gratitude. Make sure that your staff are keeping to the set hours of work and are not taking extra breaks. Make staff aware of their responsibility to achieve their targets and that you expect them to work hard and long enough to do this. If they do not, they will be failing at their job and must be disciplined or dismissed. How you get this message across is vital:

O Right from the moment you interview someone for a job you must make it quite clear that, in the final analysis, every salesperson's success is dependent not on their skills, training, or aptitude but on their attitude. *Attitude, not aptitude* – this must be your motto. Only attitude – for hard work, for persistence, for learning, for trying – will carry a trainee through their trial period and help them succeed. Make it clear that, to start with, you will judge trainees primarily on their capacity and enthusiasm for hard work. And warn trainees that if you do not think they are working hard enough, you will dismiss them. This is the only way to instil a willingness to work hard – right from the start. If you suddenly start asking people to work harder six months into their jobs you will receive a very negative and complacent response.

O Emphasize the benefits of hard work in all your advice and goal-setting. Make it your creed that if every technique to improve the *quality* of performance has been tried without success, the only approach to take is to improve the *quantity* of work:

If you can't work any smarter, work harder! Once you're working hard – then work smart!

O It follows that if you have given a salesperson every support and encouragement to perform, and they are not performing, the responsibility for their failure no longer lies with you, but with them. It is important that they understand this. In these circumstances, you must explain to salespeople that if they are not prepared to work late or work harder to achieve their goals, then they are showing themselves uncommitted to the job.

O Always include someone's enthusiasm for hard work in their reviews. Make promotions conditional on hard work.

Train people in the habit of working late, by arranging to see them for meetings outside of office hours as if this should be perfectly normal. Start your sales meetings at 8.30 and make attendance compulsory. Provided you work hard and display an enthusiasm for your work no one will become resentful – or if they do, the fault lies with them. Discipline anyone who is late directly after the meeting.

Perhaps your staff will work harder voluntarily if they understand why. It may be obvious to you, but not to them. Explain the need for extra effort (for example the recession, need to expand business, increased competition and so on) and tell them what sort of tasks you think can be accomplished before or after work, and why it will help them do better. Reward hard work with gratitude and respect.

Reinforce the need for working late by insisting that non-essential tasks are not done during prime selling time. Or set staff targets for work volume which they have to achieve before leaving.

If you are dealing with a field sales force, establish rules for when the first and last appointments of the day can be (for example the first must be no later than 9.00, the last no earlier than 4.45).

When disciplining or correcting a person who *does* work hard/late, tell them you will overlook their failings on this occasion because of the effort they put in. If you are correcting someone who does not work late, tell them that, because of this, you will not give them the benefit of the doubt.

A FINAL WORD OF CAUTION

Working longer hours is not in itself productive. If staff are forced to work late, or know they have to be seen to work late, many will deliberately drag out tasks or will spend their time doing things that do not need to be done – and feel resentful into the bargain! First of all, your staff must be motivated – and they must want to gain from the extra effort.

STAFF NOT DOING THEIR WORK THOROUGHLY

This is one of the main causes of lost orders. Salespeople miss sales through not doing their jobs thoroughly – or through doing them sloppily. Typical mistakes are:

- Not making call-backs (or not making them punctually).
- Not taking notes about a customer's wants, needs or time-scale.
- Not cold calling properly.
- Taking 'no' for an answer too readily.
- Not being inquisitive.
- Being scared of asking questions.
- Not qualifying the customer properly.
- Not having adequate systems and planning.
- Losing important documents, information.
- Not having the right address, phone number, even name, of the customer.
- Not taking a genuine interest in the customer.

There are, unfortunately, many more! In a sense, staff will always fail to do the job as thoroughly as it could, or should, be done – it is part and parcel of the sales manager's job to recognize this and keep it to a minimum.

One of the only ways to stop staff making careless or sloppy mistakes is through fear of being caught. Many staff make mistakes because they do not understand the importance of doing things correctly: if you can show them how a mistake cost them a sale, or how being thorough helped them to gain a sale, you might – just might! – make them see the error of their ways.

As sales manager, you should spend a large proportion of your time enforcing company standards and going through your staff's sales records line by line looking for errors or signs of sloppiness. Of course, you can only do this fairly if your staff have all been given:

- Clear instructions as to what level of thoroughness and administration is expected.
- Training and refresher courses.

When you discover mistakes, how can you correct them? It depends on the seriousness of the mistake, the salesperson in question and so on. Sometimes a suitable joke will do the trick. On other occasions it is best to take detailed notes of the mistake, and set the salesperson a task which they must complete within certain tight, but realistic, time-scales. For instance, if a salesperson has not been qualifying his customers properly, ask him to qualify the next seven fully, according to the questions you tell him, and show you their details as soon as he has done it. If he has not been canvassing properly instruct him to recanvass his territory, or make him canvass all day until he has achieved *twice* his average number of leads. Whatever the task set, you must be equally thorough in checking up on it, or you will be wasting your time.

Although thoroughness in everything is important, don't overdo it: concentrate on those areas of the selling process which are most likely to affect the making or losing of orders. You will lose credibility if you harangue a salesperson for not doing something everyone knows is a waste of effort.

Whenever salespeople do something 'by the book' praise them, especially when they make a sale because of it. Don't just smugly say 'I told you so'.

Are new leads being acted on quickly enough? This is a common problem. Keep a notebook of all new leads and the time they come in. Check back with staff half an hour later (or ten minutes – whatever is appropriate) – and be tough if they have done nothing. Even better, make a rule that any lead which is not worked within 10 minutes will be passed to someone else – at your discretion.

If you suspect a sale has been lost through carelessness, question the salesperson until they admit (and see for themselves) their mistake. For instance: what was the customer's budget? What was the decision-making process? Who were the decision-makers? What were they looking for? Did they have a time-scale? What was it? What other alternatives were they considering? Why? Why did they choose one of these alternatives? Does it really fit what you said they were looking for? When did you find out about their decision? Did you expect the decision then? What did you say in favour of your solution? Why didn't you inform me of this sooner?

Quizzing staff this way is sometimes the only way to make them realize their lack of knowledge about the buying process – and can sometimes uncover evidence to help you turn the sale around. As soon as you show your staff that you will not just let mistakes go, they stop making so many.

On a more positive note, you may want to award prizes for such things as the best customer file, or the best order book. You should not create a cult of tidiness for its own sake – everyone should know that the importance of thoroughness is to make more sales.

HIGH STAFF TURNOVER

As we saw in Chapter 11, there are many reasons why you can suffer from high staff turnover:

- Poor working conditions.
- No opportunity to progress/nothing to look forward to.
- No job interest.
- Poor morale.
- Unlikable management/no management.
- No opportunity to improve one's skills or prospects.
- Better jobs elsewhere.

Almost all have solutions. Here are some examples:

- Treat your staff with respect.
- When any of your staff leave find out why – could you have done anything about it?
- Give your staff short-term goals (weekly or monthly) to help them apply themselves and long-term goals (half-yearly or yearly) to maintain their interest. Six-monthly competitions are ideal. Praise everyone attaining their goals.
- Can you set up an ongoing training schedule or reward people with external training seminars at six-monthly intervals?
- Instead of raising salaries, can you offer end-of-year bonuses, based on individual or group performance?
- Can you stimulate the company's social life? Organize company nights out, or trips. Perhaps even appoint someone as entertainments officer.
- Can you create or improve the career structure? Maybe create the opportunity for staff to take part in training. Or give them overriding commission on trainees.

- Are people leaving when they find the job is much harder, or less glamorous, than they had expected? In which case you should review how you present the job at interview: do you oversell it, or don't you prepare people for how hard they must work? Perhaps you should recruit people from different backgrounds – are there any sales professions which are less 'pleasant' than yours (for instance, recruitment consultancies regularly recruit advertising sales executives, who have developed a stomach for phonework).
- What about the more obvious reasons: are you pushing your staff too hard, or criticizing them too severely, or failing to give them enough back-up or praise? Is your commission structure unfair, or ungenerous? Can people be more successful, or happier, elsewhere?
- Is your company guilty of not showing loyalty to salespeople who are having a bad month? Is this right or wrong in your market?

14

MANAGING DIFFICULT STAFF

Unfortunately, no matter how good a leader you are, and no matter how happy and motivated your team, there will be times when you have to cope with, manage, or discipline staff who are, in terms of their behaviour, attitudes or performance, 'troublesome' or 'difficult'. This chapter suggests several practical ways of dealing productively with difficult staff. It is divided into the following sections:

- Understanding difficult behaviour
- Typical problems
- Disruptive behaviour
- Discipline
- How to avoid disruptive behaviour
- Conclusion.

UNDERSTANDING DIFFICULT BEHAVIOUR

As with most problems, the best way of tackling difficult behaviour is to start by trying to understand the reason which has caused it. This will often provide you with a solution to the problem. If we consider archetypal 'difficult' behaviour (disrespect for your authority, failure to comply with your instructions, poor sales figures), all of the following might be reasons:

- Resentment: The person feels he/she is too experienced or too old to be managed by you.
- Boredom and demotivation: The person is fed up with his/her career.
- Insecurity: The person is scared of rejection and failure, and so acts in a way to actually guarantee failure and provoke your displeasure.
- Attention-seeking: The person feels happiest when he/she has 'a problem' and receives the attention and sympathy of their colleagues and manager.

These are only some of the possible interpretations. To a certain extent you will have to rely on your instinctive 'gut feel' to determine the root cause of each problem.

DECIDE HOW TO SOLVE THE PROBLEM

You must then decide to adapt your management style either to redirect or to overcome this 'difficult' behaviour (see Chapter 2 for more details on this). Sometimes the best way to manage even directly confrontational behaviour is to work *with* the person concerned and channel his/her aggression into some constructive (and probably time-consuming) task. You might try the following solutions, depending on the underlying reason:

- **Resentment:** Do they have experience which you or your team-members could draw upon? This will show your respect (vital) and make them feel they are valuable members of the team. Can you ask this person if there are areas of the job they would like to explore or develop?
- **Boredom and demotivation:** What new challenges, new territories or opportunities can you offer? Can you change their working practices? Could they become involved in training, or are there special assignments they would enjoy? Help them to concentrate on their medium-term goals – what do they want from this job and how can they achieve it?
- **Insecurity:** Review the person's performance and show them what areas they succeed in. Reassure them of your commitment to *them*. Then agree with them a set of performance-related goals they must achieve within the next one to three months. These goals don't have to be high – but they must be achieved. This person may respond well to being placed under the tutelage of an experienced salesperson.
- **Attention-seeking:** Can you solve this by taking more notice of the person? Maybe you can spend more time collecting their sales figures every day and praising them when they've done well. Perhaps this person's behaviour is indicative of the sales team as a whole: do others feel neglected? Do you spend enough time with all your staff, in goal-settings, reviews and so on, or should this be improved? If this problem is limited to this one individual, you must consider whether he/she is an asset to your team at all. Staff who want attention to this extent can undermine team morale. They often look for something to complain about, or try to convince other team-members they are 'picked on' by the manager. Agree with this person strict performance targets which must be reached.

In general these suggestions assume that the person is worth saving. Don't be too quick to threaten people with dismissal – it is the sign of a weak manager who does not value his or her staff. As the last example illustrates, you must be prepared to consider termination as a legitimate management option. Any staff you discipline must be aware that if they do not achieve the goals you have set, termination will ensue. (Refer to Chapter 5 which covers this topic in detail.)

Sometimes difficult behaviour can come from good or even high performers. In this event, you must decide whether the person wishes to confront your authority or is merely indifferent to it.

If it is the latter, you may simply have someone who needs a more 'laissez-faire' management style (providing this does not lead to resentment within the group). Allow him/her freedom to set their own goals and working practices, on condition that they let you know what these goals are, they alert you to any problems or difficulties, and they respond to your requests for information.

Anyone who is wilfully challenging your authority must be dealt with firmly. Not only is his/her behaviour unwarranted, but it will either encourage other staff to do the same, or will demotivate staff because they resent the liberties he/she is taking. In both cases your staff will lose respect for you. Tell the person exactly why you are unhappy with their behaviour and ask them to account for it. Even if they have legitimate grievances (which you may respond to), you must make it clear that they have raised these in an unacceptable way. Now tell the person exactly how you expect them to work with you in future, and get their agreement to this. Tell them that any further breach will be grounds for starting termination procedures, but if this problem is now resolved you are prepared to forget this whole issue. Stick to your word on this. If the person's conduct does not immediately change (and stay changed!), you must discipline severely and/or dismiss.

This example illustrates an important principle of management:

Laws can only be broken once they have been made.

In other words, always let your staff know what you will or won't tolerate beforehand (within reason – some actions, such as overt insubordination or rudeness to team-members, are never excusable). Then if ever these guidelines are breached, be firm in your treatment of the offender.

TYPICAL PROBLEMS

The previous section has suggested many ways of responding to difficult behaviour. In this section we will consider some of the other common problems you can have with your staff – and how you can solve them. First of all, let's consider two principles:

O   Everyone is an individual, no one is a stereotype – concentrate on each person's individual situation.
O   Sometimes *you* are part of the problem: how can you change your behaviour to prevent this problem from happening again?

PERSON SEEMS LAZY/DOESN'T WORK HARD ENOUGH

If he/she is bored or demotivated, you will find full coverage of how to deal with this in Chapter 13. But otherwise, help this person to see that their lack of work is the reason for their figures not being better. Often people who don't work hard will claim that they do: what statistics can you quote (for example number of canvassing calls) to prove otherwise? (See Chapter 8 for details on measurement.) Then set firm, precise goals for the person: number of calls, number of meetings, times of arrival and departure from the office etc. Perhaps you can utilize someone's sense of pride by asking 'Do you want me to have to discipline you as the laziest person in the team?' or 'Don't you care that everyone makes jokes about how lazy you are?' Your best hope is that the person finds that by working harder they get better results, and enjoy work more.

PERSON IS TOO AMBITIOUS

Sometimes someone treats other staff badly, or is too aggressive in his/her dealings with you. Sometimes he/she is so ambitious they want your job! Discuss their ambitions frankly with them. If they want more responsibility within the team, tell them *what* they must do to earn it, and *when* their position will be reviewed. Don't be rushed into making promises prior to the review (point out that's what the review is there for), and set the review date sufficiently far in advance (three to six months) to show you are in control. If this person wants your job, he/she is only a serious threat if you do not have the support of *your* manager. Show the person that if he/she feels ready for management, you can help them achieve it in another company or in another part of your organization. In the meantime, make it quite clear what behaviour and what levels of performance are acceptable (and formally discipline them if these are not achieved). See if you cannot re-channel this ambition into some suitable activity, such as finding new business. It is not a good idea to put an unscrupulous and ambitious person in any position where he/she might influence others, such as training, recruitment, or team-building.

PERSON MAKES SEXIST/RACIST/UNACCEPTABLE REMARKS

No modern business organization should tolerate such unprofessional behaviour. It will compromise your managerial position and the attitude, morale and ethics of everyone in your team. Such poor attitudes may mean that the salesperson loses accounts and customers, and that you are prevented from employing the best person for the job (or lose some of your best staff) if you allow this sort of behaviour. Make clear to the person what is, and is not, acceptable – and why – and be strict on this.

SLOPPINESS

Poor attention to detail, to paperwork, to timekeeping are all serious problems. Combined with poor appearance, they suggest a poor self-image which needs to be addressed if the person is going to sell effectively. Or they suggest a lack of respect for the company and the job. All staff should be given precise guidelines for administration, paperwork and so on as part of their job description. These should always be enforced, and made an essential part of your staff's reviews.

RECURRENT SICKNESS

If one of your staff is genuinely sick or has real health problems, they have a right to expect your full support and help. Your team will also expect it of you. When the salesperson is not genuinely unwell (or dramatizes what illness he/she has), you need to draw the line.

First of all, ask yourself *why*: is the person bored, or attention-seeking, or demotivated, or unhappy – and can you solve these problems? If you cannot, concentrate on the person's sales targets. Point out that no matter how often he/she is absent, these targets must be reached: if they are not, there may be grounds for dismissal. Ask the person what work they can do from home: make a point of ringing them at home to ask their advice about their clients – if they value their work, they should be only too pleased to help. Can their customers ring them? If ever you telephone and your employee is not at home, demand to see confirmation of the doctor's appointment and so on.

Perhaps you can make the person see that his/her non-attendance is letting down the team? Point out that other people have to do his/her work – and make a point of rewarding them by re-allocating key accounts. Once you make it clear that sickness is no excuse for not working, and that it will prevent that person progressing as quickly, you will reduce the attractiveness of 'taking a sicky'.

DISRUPTIVE BEHAVIOUR

In this section we review some of the problems you may encounter with specifically unruly, disobedient and confrontational behaviour. As usual, let's examine reasons for this:

- If you are new to the post, maybe certain people are resentful, or think they – or someone else – should be in your position, or don't think you are qualified for the job.
- Staff may have no respect for you.
- Staff may be dissatisfied with the company, or with things outside their control, and take this out on you.
- Staff may resent being told to improve or change their working habits.
- A salesperson may have a grudge about anyone in authority.
- Staff may not take their work seriously.
- Staff may be bored or demotivated.
- A salesperson might be afraid of failure and want to conceal this.
- You might be behaving pompously or arrogantly.

○ Staff might be immature.
○ Staff might not be properly trained.

Once you can identify the root cause of the problem, the solution usually presents itself.

Sometimes, as you can see, staff behave badly because the sales manager is too *serious* – salespeople respect managers who have a sense of humour and are quick-witted. In these instances, try to be more 'street-wise'; maybe crack jokes to get your point across (though don't be sarcastic!); show humour when disciplining people for minor shortcomings; liven things up a bit.

Sometimes bad behaviour arises because staff do not respect and fear the sales manager, or have no respect for their jobs or their company. The following are actions you should never tolerate:

○ Showing disrespect to you, the company, a customer, or a colleague.
○ Disregarding any important aspect of the job description or the daily structure.
○ Any serious breach of trust.
○ Disruptive behaviour or lack of work.
○ Any form of prejudicial attitude.

Never let a member of staff openly disobey you, or flaunt their disrespect for you: once you allow this, you are inviting others to do the same. The secret to discipline in these instances is in:

1. Having a strong sense of self-respect, which you communicate to others.
2. Having a strong sense of respect for the company, your work and your products.
3. Making it clear exactly where you draw the line (this should also be spelt out in your staff's job descriptions).
4. Making it clear what will happen to those who cross this line.
5. Enforcing the fourth point consistently and, if necessary, ruthlessly.

There is an old management myth about neutralizing a troublemaker by promoting him into a position of authority. This rarely, if ever, works: chances are that the reasons for this person's troublemaking will still be there, only you will find it harder to criticize them and they will have an even greater influence on other members of staff. What you might do, if someone is continually complaining about a particular matter, is give that person the task of coming up with a solution.

DISCIPLINE

For additional information on disciplining staff, see Chapter 5. However, these points are specific to bad or disruptive behaviour:

1. Always make sure you stay in control of the situation. Unless you are sure of yourself and your position, do not discipline people in public – it can lead to resentment from the person, embarrassment from the rest of the staff, and you also run the risk of the matter getting out of hand. Always discipline in private, in your office. By simply telling the person to see you in your office straight away you will show that you are in control. Discipline people one at a time.
2. Once in your office tell the person exactly why you are angry, or displeased. Never beat about the bush.
3. Depending on the circumstances, you may ask them to explain themselves, or ask why they have said or done whatever they have said/done.
4. Don't accept any half-baked answer or excuse: tell them they have done wrong and you will not have them doing so again.

5 Be prepared to listen, but remember: even a reasonable explanation doesn't excuse unreasonable behaviour.
6 Never argue with the person, or become involved in a debate: you are the person's manager, and in all issues to do with misbehaviour, your word is final.
7 It may help if you explain why the person's behaviour is unacceptable. Perhaps it sets a bad example for junior, more impressionable members of staff, or is rude, or contradicts company policy, or is disruptive. Make it clear that whatever personal views a person may have, they must never be aired in public. If a person's behaviour is plainly wrong, no explanation should be necessary and you will seem weak if you offer one.
8 Don't threaten needlessly and don't overdiscipline: this will make you look foolish. If the person apologizes for a minor breach, accept it gracefully but insist it must not happen again. If the person's behaviour was more serious, so that any repeat will forfeit his/her position, you must spell this out. And if the person's behaviour was particularly bad, an apology may not be enough: dismissal may still be correct, or you might issue a letter of formal warning – which you can withdraw if the person improves.
9 Be sure of your right to discipline: never apologize or hesitate or have second thoughts – all these are signs of weakness.
10 Finally, convince the person that what they have done is wrong (provided this seems sensible).

NOTE ON DISCIPLINARY PROCEDURES

Many companies have standard disciplinary procedures with which all disciplinary actions must comply. In large companies this is the best way of ensuring fairness, impartiality and compliance with the law. In smaller companies such a process can seem needlessly pedantic. Also, discipline in sales is in some ways a special case, as such factors as attitude and behaviour are so much more important to success.

HOW TO AVOID DISRUPTIVE BEHAVIOUR

You will have fewer problems with people's behaviour if you bear the following in mind:

- Never bully people or treat them like underlings.
- Show respect.
- Don't be gullible or willing to put up with nonsense.
- Have a sense of humour.
- Only ask what is sensible: never waste people's time on pointless tasks.
- Explain the reasons for your directives, and if possible, show the benefits.
- Involve staff in deciding or implementing actions.
- Be clear about what you want done.
- Keep records – don't let people catch you out.
- Set deadlines for work – and be back at the deadline.
- Praise good work – never praise undeserving work.
- Demand an explanation for poor work.
- Reimpose tasks if necessary.

Remember: people are more likely to misbehave if you treat them like schoolchildren.

If you find it continually difficult to maintain order, this could be simply because you have too many people to keep an eye on. Solve this by developing a better structure within the team, with group leaders who are accountable for ensuring that people do their work.

CONCLUSION

As this chapter shows, there is never one solution to difficult behaviour. A few general principles can be used to sum up:

- Where does the cause lie: in the person, in the team, in your style of management, in the company?
- How can the problem be solved without diminishing your authority?
- Always act with respect for yourself, your company and your staff.
- Never permit any action or attitude which does not share this respect.
- Retain personal control of the disciplinary process.
- Discipline firmly, consistently and without hesitation.
- Do not overdiscipline or victimize.
- Retain a sense of humour!

CONCLUSION

There is no one secret to improving your team's sales performance. Each of the techniques and approaches described in this book will contribute to your success. But to be most effective they need to be applied in combination, as part of an overall, coherent strategy. In this last chapter, we will summarize and co-ordinate the key points of an effective sales leadership strategy as well as suggesting some areas for future thought.

We will start by reviewing the findings of a recent survey of top-performing sales teams. This survey sought to identify the ten most important factors in making a successful sales force. Its results were as follows:

1 Reputation among customers
2 Retaining old accounts
3 Quality of management
4 Ability to keep high performers
5 Product and technical knowledge
6 Innovation
7 Quality of training
8 Winning new customers
9 Achieving targets
10 Effectiveness and frequency of customer service.

I would add four other key factors:

- Ability to compete and win
- Greater belief in company and mission
- Quality of sales skills
- High morale and motivation.

It is a good exercise for sales managers to regularly review these fourteen points and gauge how their sales teams perform. If your team rates highly in all of these areas, it is probably already a highly successful, highly motivated team. If it is not, it soon will be.

Fundamentally, the secret of successful, really successful, sales management is this: have clear goals, have a clear sense of how to achieve them, and inspire others to share in your vision, and you are three-quarters of the way there. The rest depends on sales ability, administration, customer service, and training, training, training.... What follows is merely an expansion of this:

UNDERSTAND YOUR LEADERSHIP ROLE

Understand what you need to achieve and how you can lead your team to achieve this goal. Know your own authority and when and how to assert it.

DO NOT BE AFRAID OF DECISIONS

Accept that every decision is a risk, that any failure will be your responsibility, and that every success is usually attributed to anything and everyone but the sales manager. But it is your role to give your staff clear directions, to make and implement changes, to anticipate the market and to keep your staff one step ahead of your customers and your competitors.

PULL, DON'T PUSH

The most basic premise of motivation: dedicate yourself to understanding how you can stimulate and appeal to your salespeople's needs.

GIVE YOUR STAFF CLEAR GOALS

Set examples and standards and demand that they are maintained. Give each member of your team clear performance targets and help them achieve these.

MONITOR CLOSELY

The secret of helping your staff make more sales is in the detail: keep an eye on your staff's daily activities, their phonework, their meetings, their presentations. Help them get each step right, and don't let them sweep their mistakes under the carpet. If you don't take their work seriously, they won't.

PRAISE AND CRITICIZE

Always praise and congratulate – but only for specific achievements. Criticize as well, but only constructively.

ALWAYS TRY TO IMPROVE SKILLS

Training is fundamental to a sales team's success. Training gives them the means, know-how and confidence to turn their intentions into results. If you don't train your staff regularly and enthusiastically, they will think you don't care.

RAISE EXPECTATIONS – AND SALES

Through goal-setting, training and your belief in your staff, instil the self-confidence and ambition to succeed.

IMPROVE EFFICIENCY THROUGH COMPUTERIZATION

Modern computer systems enable you to give your customers a more efficient and personal service than was ever previously possible. And they give you the opportunity to monitor and analyse the work of every salesperson.

RECRUIT THE RIGHT QUALITY OF SALESPERSON

Any organization with a long-term record of growth and success has a coherent, quality-orientated recruitment and induction programme. Almost all believe in training at least a proportion of their sales staff from scratch. All have a strong and positive company culture.

GIVE YOUR WORKING ENVIRONMENT A CLEAR SENSE OF STRUCTURE

Job descriptions, sales manuals, scheduled sales meetings, training sessions, reviews, promotions, goal-settings, daily work routines – all of these are necessary for your staff to develop a strong sense of order, purpose and pride in their work.

REWARD HIGH PERFORMANCE FINANCIALLY AND PERSONALLY

You will never get your staff to out-perform mediocrity unless you pay them to. Ensure your commission structures adequately repay high and above-average performance. But don't just concentrate on money: make your staff feel valued as people with promotions, prizes and praise.

STRIVE TO IMPROVE THE QUALITY OF YOUR CUSTOMER SERVICE

Customer service starts with the quality of your brochures and letterheads, and the quality of the initial canvass call. It is present in the quality of your staff's appearance, and the relevance and suitability of their solutions. It is evident in the care and quality of their presentations and proposals. It is there in the terms of the contract and the punctual delivery of the finished product. But it is most conspicuous in the care you take with your customers after they have bought.

KEEP AHEAD OF THE FIELD

You can never afford to rest on your laurels. You can never afford to stick with a winning combination. You must always try to innovate, improve, offer greater flexibility, greater service, better products. If you don't, your competitors will.

AND FINALLY... ENJOY YOURSELF!

Sales management is probably the most demanding and challenging managerial function in modern business. It calls for a wider range of personal qualities and skills than any other equivalent role, and more immediately affects the success or failure of the company as a whole. To be a successful sales manager, you must understand and satisfy the needs of your customers, your staff and your superiors as well as fulfil your own personal goals – and not only satisfy these needs, but predict and anticipate them and lead your staff into the uncharted territory of the future, for nothing is ever certain in sales.

Sales management offers tremendous scope for leadership, innovation and achievement, and sometimes even gratitude. Be proud of your ability and your opportunity and enjoy every minute of it!

INDEX

achievement theory, 31–2
administration, 8–10, 35, 48, 77–84, 112, 131
    administration for canvassing, 86
    assessing administration, 77–8
    improving administration, 78–83
    see also organization, records
advertising (to recruit), 98–99
advertising (products/company), 115
advice, 6
analysing performance, 39, 42, 65–75
    an example, 71
    by ratio, 69–71
    by volume, 69–70
appearance (manager's), 9, 54
application form (for recruiting), 104
appraisals, see reviews
assessing performance, 42–3, 65–75
    an example, 71
    assessing administration, 77–8
    assessing qualitative data, 72
    assessing successfully, 68
    assessing to improve performance, 72, 73–5
    by ratio, 69–71
    by volume, 69–70
    staff self-assessment, 73–5
    what to assess, 65–67
attention-seeking behaviour (in staff), 28, 45, 123–4, 126
attitude (positive, of staff), 35, 43, 48, 96–7, 106–8, 117–9, 128
attribution theory, 31–2
authority (manager's), 7, 16, 117–9, 124, 126–7

beating competition, 85–90, 112–5, 120
    see also customers
belief (in company), 3, 22, 113, 131–3
boosting sales, 113–5
    see also improving performance, beating competition
boredom (in staff), 95, 123, 124, 126
bully (role), 29

canvassing, 38, 72, 86, 114–15
    see also cold-calling
care for loved ones, 23
career path (staff's), 48–51, 95, 106, 120

carelessness (staff's), 119–20
    see also sloppiness
change
    communicating change, 5, 18, 53, 56–7
    implementing change, 18, 38, 54–7
    managing change, 17–18
    using change, 112, 133
    see also sales meetings, guardian of the norms
cold-calling, 50, 62, 117
    see also canvassing
comfort (need for), 23
commission schemes, 15, 31, 36, 59–62, 106, 114, 120, 133
commitment (staff's, to company, to work etc.), 3, 17–18, 41–3, 47–8, 61, 73
communication skills, 4, 6, 53–8, 128
    communicating goals, 15, 53, 67–8
    see also goal-setting, discipline, reviews, sales meetings, memos
competition (from other companies) see beating competition
competitions, 31, 62–3, 112, 116, 120
competitive spirit, 26
complaints (staff's), 45–46
complaints (customers'), 34, 87, 90–91
computers, 68, 82–3, 86, 90, 132
conditions (working conditions), 31, 95, 112
critic (role), 28
criticism (giving to staff), 5, 31, 42, 45, 57, 120, 132
    see also motivation, pride, praise
customers,
    customer service, 34–5, 49, 85–92, 94, 131–3
    customer service questionnaire, 88–90, 114
    improving customer service, 85–92
    targeting customers, 87–8, 114–15

deadlines (using effectively), 44, 47–8, 80–81, 119, 128
delegation, 80
    see also group-leaders, leadership styles, promotion, structure (hierarchy)
demoralization (in staff), 57, 61–2, 94, 111–13, 120, 123
desire for praise (staff's), 27
    see also praise
desire to be helpful (staff's), 26
    see also Helper (role)

desire to be liked (staff's), 26
difficult staff (managing difficult staff), 18–19, 57–8, 113, 117–19, 123–9
discipline (use of), 7, 28–9, 36–7, 44, 46–8, 66, 68, 113–14, 117–19, 124–5, 127–9
   prizes used to discipline, 62
dismissing staff, 28–9, 47, 94–6, 118–19, 124
disruptive behaviour (managing), 126–7
   see also difficult staff
duties (staff's), 34
   see also job description

ease, 27
evaluating performance *see* assessing performance
excitement, 27, 115
expectancy theory, 31, 43, 114
expectations (staff's), 37, 49, 113, 132

failure (staff failure), 95–6
falling sales, 113–15
fear (use of), 27
feedback, 53–4, 75
   see also communication skills, criticism, praise
figure-taking, 38–9, 65, 68–70, 78, 81–2, 90
   see also records, administration

goal-setting, 33, 36–7, 41–4, 47–8, 54, 67, 75, 113–14, 117, 124–5, 132–3
   see also goals, targets
goals, 2, 3, 5, 6, 27, 31, 33, 34, 66, 117, 120, 131
   communicating goals, 13 (*see also* communication skills)
   goal-assessment, 11
   managing by goals, 11–13
   personal goals, 12–13
   team-goals, 14–15
   see also goal-setting, targets
greed, 23, 26
grievances, 45–6, 57, 124
   see also complaints (staff's)
group-leaders, 50, 78–9, 104, 108, 112, 128
guardian of the norms, 28, 57

habit, 26
hard work (getting staff to work hard), 3, 111–13, 115–20, 125
helper (role), 29
Herzberg's theory, 31
high-performers, 26, 31, 60, 93–4, 115–16, 124, 131, 133
humour, *see* sense of humour

improving performance (implicit throughout *Leading the Sales Team*, but points of interest are), 42–4, 48–9, 50–1, 55, 59–60, 68, 72–3, 75, 78, 82–3, 85–92, 112–16, 120, 131–3
   see also boosting sales, beating competition, commission schemes, competitions
incentives, 62
   see also commission schemes, competitions, prizes
inconsistent results, 62
innovator (role), 28
insecurity (in staff, sources of etc.), 24, 28, 45–6, 94, 123, 126
interest, 26

interviewing, 34, 100, 103–8, 118
   how to interview, 105–8
   planning interviews, 103–4
   telephone interviews, 99

job description, 33–7, 49, 50, 66–7, 97, 105–6, 126–7, 133
job satisfaction (staff's), 48–9, 56, 95, 120
joker (role), 28

leadership (implicit throughout *Leading the Sales Team*, points of interest as follows), 1–19, 22, 131–3
   definition of, 1–2
   four sources of, 2–10
   goals, 2, 3, 5
   leadership by example, 113–14, 116–17
   personal qualities involved, 2–4
   position within organization, 7–8, 125
   relationship with staff, 4–7
   strategy, 131–33
   styles of, 5, 6, 16–17, 123–4
   ways of working, 8–10
   see also motivation, time-management, communication skills, goals, goal-setting, organization, administration, poor management
leads (business), *see* new leads
loner (role), 28
losing staff, 95
   see also turnover
loyalty (staff's), 26, 47–8, 61, 63

management *see* leadership, administration, organization, monitoring performance, assessing performance, evaluating performance, difficult staff, troubleshooting, time-management, records, figure-taking, recruiting, delegation, poor management
manual *see* sales manual
Maslow, 30–31
meeting, *see* sales meetings
memos, 54
monitoring performance, 31, 38–9, 68–75, 82, 86, 114, 132
   see also figure-taking, records, assessing performance, evaluating performance
morale, 14, 33, 35, 37, 48–50, 83, 94, 111–14, 124, 131
   see also motivation, demoralization
motivation, 21–32, 95, 112–13, 116, 121, 131–2
   analysing needs, 24–5
   introduction to, 21–2
   motivating through organization *see* Chapters 4, 5 and 7
   motivation theories, 30–2
   theory of roles, 27–30
   understanding needs, 22–7, 123, 132
   see also job description, sales manual, goal-setting, discipline, praise, criticism, promotions, sales meetings, improving performance, commission schemes, competitions, prizes, respect
motivator–hygiene theory, 31

needs (motivational) *see* motivation, Maslow
new leads (business), 38, 49–50, 75, 85–92, 114–16, 119–20, 125
   see also cold-calling

INDEX

organization, 8–10, 33, 77–84
  see also administration, job description, sales manual, goal-setting, sales meetings, motivation, discipline, promotions, structure, time-management, commission schemes
offers (making offers of employment), 109

pay, 23–4, 26, 31, 59–62, 95, 97
payrises, 23–24
peace of mind, 23–4
peer-group pressure, 23, 25
pep-talk, 112–13
performance see assessing performance, monitoring performance, improving performance, analysing performance
poor management (mistakes in management are considered throughout *Leading the Sales Team*, but see particularly), 3–4, 27, 111, 116–17, 124–7, 129
power, 26
praise, 5, 15, 27, 31, 42, 44–5, 48, 56, 68, 95, 117, 120, 128, 132–3
  see also criticism, communication skills
prestige (company's), 36, 88–9, 104–5
pricing, 92, 115
pride, 23, 25, 125, 133
priorities (staff's), 6, 34–8, 60, 87–8
prioritization (management), 8–9, 11–13, 60, 75, 78–81, 87–8, 110
prizes, 62–3, 112, 120, 133
  ideas for, 63
problem-child (role), 28
promotions, 48–9, 66
  see also group-leaders, structure (hierarchy)
psychometric testing, 24, 73, 108–9

qualitative data, 66, 72, 114
qualities for sales success, 96–7, 131
quantitative data, 65–6, 68–71
questionnaires,
  customer service, 88–90, 114
  staff self-assessment, 73–5

racism, 126
rebel-leader (role), 29
recession, 113–15
records, 8–10, 35, 39, 41, 68–70, 72, 81–2, 86, 91, 110, 119, 128
  putting records to work, 81–2
  see also figure-taking, monitoring performance, assessing performance
recruiting, 66–7, 93–110, 120, 132
  advertising, 98–9
  agencies, 99–100
  identifying recruitment requirements, 96–7
  school-leavers, 100–101
  the recruitment specification, 97
  through referrals, 100
  see also interviewing, references, offers, rejections, sales ability, qualities for sales success
references (taking up references), 108
referrals (new business), 90
rejections (making rejections), 109–110
reports, 35
resentment (in staff, sources of etc.), 25–8, 45–6, 50, 69, 83, 117–19, 123–4, 126–7

respect (treating staff with), 4–7, 27, 49–50, 116–17, 120, 124, 129
reviews (performance and/or salary), 36, 43–5, 49, 54, 75, 125, 133
  reviewing applicants for employment, 106–7
  reviewing work-in-progress, 82
  see also goal-setting
rewards, 7, 31, 48, 59–63, 95, 117, 120
roles (theory of), 27–30

sales ability (criteria for), 66–7, 72, 96–7, 106–107, 114
sales forecasting see assessing performance, figure-taking, goal-setting, records
sales manual, 31, 36–7, 67, 133
sales meetings, 15, 35, 50, 53–8, 67, 89, 112, 133
  see also pep-talk, communication skills
sales proposals, 78–9
sales skills, for a full treatment of sales skills and techniques, consult *Training the Sales Team*.
sales targets see targets
school-leavers, 100–101
security (staff's need for), 26
senior staff see group-leaders
sense of humour, 127–9
sergeant-major (role), 29
sickness (recurrent), 126
sloppiness, 126
  see also carelessness
specialization, 80, 86–7
staff problems see difficult staff, disruptive behaviour, motivation, poor management, troubleshooting
standardization, 80
standards (of performance), 34, 37, 67–8, 72, 119, 125–6
  see also goal-setting, job description, sales manual, sales targets
structure (hierarchy), 36, 49–51, 106, 128, 133
structure (daily working structure), 31, 37–8, 55, 81, 83, 106, 114, 133

targets (sales targets), 36, 41–3, 113–15, 126
  see also goal-setting, goals, commission schemes
task-setting, 4–6, 11–13, 17, 21, 25, 31, 41–3, 80, 116–20, 123, 128
  see also deadlines, goal-setting
teaching aids, prizes as teaching aids, 62
  see also training
team, 14–16, 105–6
  building the sales team, 14–16, 96, 131
  benefits of the team, 14
  motivating the team, 29
  team-goals, 14–15
  team-structure, 15, 36, 49–51 (see, structure)
  see also morale, roles (theory of), leadership, sales meetings, difficult staff, motivation
team-player (role), 28
team-spirit see morale
time-management, 8–9, 38, 77–81, 87–8, 118
timescales (using effectively) see deadlines
training, for a full treatment of training, see *Training the Sales Team*. Main points within this book are, 15, 18, 34–5, 37, 44, 50, 66, 75, 95, 106, 112, 114, 116–17, 119, 131–3
troubleshooting, 111–29
  demoralization, 111–13
  falling sales, 113–15
  high staff turnover, 93–6, 120–21
  staff not working hard enough, 116–19

staff not working thoroughly, 119–120
too few high-performers, 115–16
see also difficult staff, disruptive behaviour
turnover (high staff turnover), 93–6, 120–1

unique selling points, 112

weak management *see* poor management
weakling (role), 28

Expand!
The Dynamic Approach to International Marketing Development

Alain-Eric Giordan

With contributions by Sir Adrian Cadbury

Giordan describes how expanding international market share is within the capacity of any company of any size. In his best selling, prizewinning book, now available in English for the first time, he shows how to take a fresh approach to export markets. Sound advice on identifying your own strengths and weaknesses, and matching them with market characteristics and opportunities, is combined with over 500 short case studies demonstrating the full range of dynamic devices, and some of the personal successes and failures of more than 150 companies worldwide.

For example the book describes:

- How Kellogg rechristened Bran Buds in Sweden, where its literal translation is 'grilled farmer'.
- How Lacoste suffered counterfeiting in Brazil, entered the market, and took it by storm.
- How Hewlett Packard exported their "HP Way" to 70 countries.
- How Club Med changed Japanese attitudes to taking holidays.
- How a leading yogurt brand increases sales by adapting it regionally to suit local tastes for sweetness.

Expand! will help any company devise a realistic international strategy, and implement it through a 'cocktail' of dynamic devices which are 'mixed' to suit both company and market. The whole range of both market-push and market-pull techniques are described, together with product related approaches that will combine to increase competitive edge.

Any company keen to expand and energize its worldwide development will find *Expand!* an essential handbook.

| 1994 | 448 pages | 0 566 07435 4 |

Gower

Licensing
The International Sale of Patents and Technical Knowhow

Michael Z Brooke and John M Skilbeck

This book is designed to take the reader through the maze of activities necessary for the successful selling of technical expertise internationally. It provides a comprehensive review of licensing for the practitioner: how and where licensing is used, the kinds of business supported, the opportunities, the problems and their solutions, together with other relevant issues.

After Part 1, which summarizes current usage, Part 2 examines the strategic aspects of licensing as a method of operating outside the home country; the relevant decisions are listed as are other options such as investment and franchising. In Part 3 the authors turn to legal and political issues and include a specimen agreement. Part 4 deals with the managerial issues – including organizing, planning, financing, marketing and staffing – and concludes by examining the vexed question of relationships between licensor and licensee. Part 5 looks at special considerations for particular nations and regions (including the developing world) while Part 6 summarizes and looks to the future.

The result is a comprehensive and up-to-date view of the issues and questions that face the licensing executive, together with practical guidance on dealing with these issues effectively.

| 1994 | 450 pages | 0 566 07461 3 |

Sales Promotion in Postmodern Marketing

Christian Petersen and Alan Toop

In this challenging new book the authors argue for a radical review of sales promotion practice. All the circumstances that led to the evolution of modern marketing have changed prodigiously: consumer spending patterns are different; the mass markets of the 1960s and 1970s have fragmented. Less is being spent on advertising and more on sales promotion and direct mail. Above all, today's consumer is more individual, more assertive – and more sceptical.

According to the authors these developments will make successful brands ever more valuable. But success will require a different approach to what actually constitutes a brand, and a more subtle and flexible use of a wide range of media and methods to communicate brand values. Much of the book is devoted to a searching examination of non-advertising sales promotion techniques. The media and the methods are reviewed in detail to show how each of them can be deployed to maximum effect, and in a final section the management implications are considered.

The text is designed to give practical guidance and is illustrated throughout by examples of successful campaigns drawn from several countries and a wide variety of businesses.

| 1994 | 206 pages | 0 566 07450 8 |